THE GEOFF PLUMB COLLECTION

BRITISH RAILWAYS IN THE 1960s

SOUTHERN REGION

THE GEOFF PLUMB COLLECTION

BRITISH RAILWAYS IN THE 1960s

SOUTHERN REGION

GEOFF PLUMB

PEN & SWORD TRANSPORT

First published in Great Britain in 2017 by
Pen & Sword Transport
An imprint of Pen & Sword Books Ltd
47 Church Street
Barnsley
South Yorkshire
S70 2AS

ISBN 9781473823938

Typeset by Pen & Sword Books Ltd
Printed and bound in India by Replika Press Pvt. Ltd.

Typeset in Palatino

Pen & Sword Books Ltd incorporates the imprints of Pen & Sword
Archaeology, Atlas, Aviation, Battleground, Discovery, Family History,
History, Maritime, Military, Naval, Politics, Railways, Select, Social
History, Transport, True Crime, and Claymore Press, Frontline Books,
Leo Cooper, Praetorian Press, Remember When, Seaforth Publishing
and Wharncliffe.

For a complete list of Pen and Sword titles please contact
Pen and Sword Books Limited
47 Church Street, Barnsley, South Yorkshire, S70 2AS, England
E-mail: enquiries@pen-and-sword.co.uk
Website: www.pen-and-sword.co.uk

Frontispiece
From the Geoff Plumb Collection. From left to right, author Geoff
Plumb, together with younger brothers Barry and Keith Plumb, pose
with LSWR C14 Class 0-4-0T No. 77s between its duties shunting at
Southampton Town Quay (Queen's Quay) on Saturday 14 June 1958.

The loco was rebuilt in 1918 from an earlier 2-2-0T built in 1906
by Drummond, so it wasn't as ancient as it looked! It was resident
shunter at the Redbridge Sleeper Works for many years but when
classmates 30588 and 30589 were withdrawn in 1957 (December
and June respectively) and replaced by diesel power in the docks
(Drewry 204bhp 0-6-0DM No. 11223), clearance problems were
immediately apparent. So 77s was borrowed from Redbridge and
worked on the dock intermittently for lengthy periods between
December 1957 and 10 February 1959.

Drewry No. 11224, which had cutback footsteps to aid clearances,
became available from 12 January 1959, but a manning dispute
meant 77s doing the honours for a short while once more. It was
withdrawn from service on 21 March 1959 and scrapped at Eastleigh
Works on 2 May 1959. Photo taken by my father, Derek Plumb,
using the family Box Brownie camera.

INTRODUCTION

AS I WAS BORN and brought up in Sheffield, Yorkshire, it may seem strange that the first in this series of books covers the Southern area of Britain's railways, but there are sound reasons for this.

I regard myself as being extremely lucky as a member of the last generation to be born into an era when the railways in the British Isles were still almost exclusively steam operated, though sadly steam breathed its last gasp in normal use on British Railways before I was out of my teenage years. Steam soldiered on in industrial use, also with a few survivors flying the flag with London Transport and in Northern Ireland, very much a rear-guard action.

I was also very lucky in having an avid railway enthusiast as my father – Derek Plumb – his own interest being kindled around the age of twelve years in the mid-1930s, upon his first sighting of a new LMS Maroon 5XP 'Jubilee' at Sheffield Midland station. He and his elder brother, Ken, soon discovered the delights of the 'Plant' at Doncaster, which they visited frequently on their bikes, to see newly built Gresley A4 'Streamliners', as well as older types such as the Great Northern 'Atlantics'.

Sheffield, of course, had a wealth of former Great Central and Midland Railway engines going about their daily tasks, together with newer LNER and LMS classes. However, on what became frequent marathon bicycle trips to far flung places around the country, my father discovered and fell in love with everything to do with the LNWR, following visits to Crewe and Chester. These activities were rather curtailed by the onset of the Second World War, though the interest was kept up through railway travels in connection with my father's work prior to being called-up.

Even then, much of the training he had to do involved railways to a great extent, and eventually he ended up in India with the Royal Engineers, just as the war was coming to an end. Having been heavily involved with the building and testing of a Military Refrigeration Unit train, he spent some time based opposite the engine sheds in Jhansi, where he was able to conduct many footplate trips with the blessing of the local railway authorities.

Perhaps like many other couples in those uncertain times, Derek and my mother, Margaret, were married when they were just 19 years old. The wedding was in September 1943, and they managed a week's honeymoon in Colwyn Bay, travelling by train, of course, from Sheffield. My sister, Gwyneth, was the first of their children on the scene, in 1945, by which time Derek was in India and did not return until 1947.

I was born at home in Gleadless, Sheffield, in March 1949 and my brothers, Barry and Keith, followed in 1950 and 1953 respectively, so the family was complete while my parents were still relatively young and active.

Derek's railway interests continued to flourish and in the pursuit of greater knowledge he became a member of the Railway Correspondence & Travel Society (RCTS), and on enquiring why there was no Sheffield branch of the society was informed that if he wanted one, then start one!

So, 1950 saw the inauguration of that branch and railway activities increased; my own first visit with the branch being to Immingham depot, amongst others, in 1951. Derek had realised that by not starting his own interest until almost a teenager, he had missed seeing a tremendous variety of ancient surviving engines that had been replaced by more modern types and he was determined that I, and subsequently my brothers, would not miss anything that was still around when we were very small.

Thus, we spent a great deal of our time on 'shed bashes' with the Sheffield RCTS, often by the means of Booth & Fisher road coaches, on railtours and outings organised by many other branches and, of course, independent trips, days out and family holidays. Perhaps my mother and sister might have preferred the occasional holiday that didn't involve railways to a greater or lesser extent, but they rarely got the chance!

Much time was also spent on the platforms at Sheffield Midland and Victoria stations, train watching sessions at Bernard Road overlooking both the former Great Central and Midland lines and out in the Peak District and Pennines.

Family holiday favourite destinations were North Wales, occasionally Devon and the Isle of Wight. This always made a great impression, simply because you had to take a boat trip to get there, so it seemed exotically different.

The railways there were a delight of ancient rolling stock and locos, running through lovely countryside where it always appeared to be sunny and warm and so the former Southern Railway made a deep impact in one's affection.

Even in the mid-fifties people had to be prepared to move to new locations in order to advance in their careers, and this was the case with my father. He had started as an apprentice at Brightside Engineering as a fourteen-year-old and had become well qualified in the Heating, Ventilation and Refrigeration field, especially after his training for military duties. He had always had a 'roving commission' working on development sites all over the country, and this fostered his enthusiasm for travel by train. By the mid-fifties though, he was working at a small heating company located in Meadowhall but was offered a much better job with G.N. Haden & Sons Ltd, based in their London offices adjacent to the canal backing onto the famous Gasworks between St Pancras and King's Cross stations.

So for a while Derek lodged with RCTS friends living in Disraeli Road, Putney, their garden backing onto the Southern Railway line near Putney station and the bridge that carried the District line over it. Eventually, a suitable house was found for the family in Harrow Weald and so in 1957, when I was aged eight, it was a case of up sticks and move south (by train, of course!) to a different life.

Where we moved to was just a short walk to the West Coast Main Line where the first diesels were beginning to make their presence felt, but goods trains could still be seen behind LNWR 'Super D' 0-8-0s, while Stanier's designs were still predominant on the expresses. From my primary school in Belmont it was possible to hear the local branch train from Harrow & Wealdstone, often operated by Fowler 3MT 2-6-2T No. 40010. Watford shed also had its own pet LMS 2P 4-4-0 No. 40672, frequently seen pottering about.

We spent many an evening over at Hadley Wood on the East Coast Main Line, where the new tunnels were under construction to allow four tracks and double the capacity of the former bottleneck north of Greenwood to Potter's Bar.

Here of course expresses were in the hands of Gresley Pacifics of one sort or another, together with their later Thompson and Peppercorn cousins.

Despite his deep interest in railways, my father had never progressed beyond having a Kodak Box Brownie camera, as taking photos was not his forte – it went on holidays with us and plenty of family pictures were taken, but only the occasional shot of trains. It could, of course, only cope with static shots in any case, as the shutter speed meant moving trains were most likely to be blurred. Nevertheless, the camera fascinated me and I liked to peer through the rather primitive viewfinder at a fairly distorted view of the world.

Thus, on one of our many trips on railtours I begged to borrow the camera and took my own first photograph – of a Southern Railway engine, former LBSCR Class H2 Atlantic No. 32424 *Beachy Head* at the end of its final run to Newhaven in April 1958 on the RCTS 'Sussex Coast Railtour'. Not a brilliant photo but a passable effort!

It wasn't until a couple of years later, in May 1960, that I got another opportunity when I was on a primary school geography field trip, when the party stayed for a few days in Swanage. This involved a couple of trips from Wareham to Swanage on the branch auto-train, operated by a Southern M7 0-4-4T, and I even managed a shot of a moving train through Poole station with a rebuilt Bulleid Pacific in charge – quite an achievement!

There was also a visit to Weymouth, where I was lucky enough to get a photo of one of the outside cylinder 'Pannier Tanks' on the Quay Tramway, though sadly this was on a fairly dull day.

By some fluke, I managed to pass my 11-plus exams and started at Harrow Weald County Grammar School in September 1960. The school had an extensive library and I soon discovered it had several books on photography, which I gradually worked my way through, taking in as much information as possible. My ambition was now to get a camera of my own, and at last the opportunity arose when I was asked by my parents what I would like for my thirteenth birthday in March 1962.

The answer, of course, was 'a camera, please!', though my expectations were to receive perhaps a slightly better version of the family Box Brownie, if I were lucky.

Not knowing much about the subject himself, my father

consulted family friend and RCTS member John Edgington – an accomplished photographer – for advice. John took Derek off to Brunnings Camera Exchange in Holborn, Derek telling John that the most he could run to was £5. After some rummaging around, John came up with a second-hand 120 roll film folding camera for the princely sum of £4 12s, telling Derek that this would give me a challenge and foster my interest much more than a glorified box camera.

You can imagine my delight at getting this – something way beyond my wildest dreams! It was a Voigtländer Perkeo I with f3.5 Color-Skopar 80mm lens and Prontor shutter, and it took 12 x 2¼in square pictures on a roll of 120 size film.

Just a few days after my birthday the camera had its first outing, its first subject for me being 'Britannia' class Pacific No. 70003 *John Bunyan* at the head of the RCTS 'Great Eastern Commemorative Railtour' from London Liverpool Street to Norwich, and then on a wander round various branch lines with GER J17 0-6-0 No. 65567.

This then became the start of something of a mad rush to get as many photos as possible as steam locos were beginning to disappear at an alarming rate – I had already missed the last workings of the Stanier 'Princess Royal' Pacifics on the WCML, the 'Kings' had finished on the Great Western while the 'Lord Nelsons' and 'King Arthurs' had gone from the Southern. Within fifteen months or so, regular steam workings south of Peterborough to King's Cross had finished, so it was already a struggle.

There was also the 'Catch 22' situation of being a fulltime schoolboy, meaning it was not possible to get out during the week, and it was difficult to meet the expense of buying film and getting it processed as I had no means of doing this myself. I was doing anything up to three paper-rounds each morning prior to going to school and at weekends, together with working in a local greengrocer's shop one afternoon and evening after school and also on Saturdays. Thus, I could run to buying the film but had little time in which to use it!

Fortunately, we were still getting out on tours and visits, both organised and also family events and holidays. This usually meant I had to try and find someone to fill-in for me with the part-time jobs, making things something of a logistical nightmare.

I did, however, manage to get quite a lot of material in black and white and even managed to put a couple of colour films (Kodak Ektachrome – 32 asa!) through the camera, though not with brilliant results. Mostly I used Ilford HP3 film, rated at 400 asa, meaning I could use a fast shutter speed for moving trains (though the fastest shutter speed was 1/300 second, so could still result in blurring with a speeding train), the downside being that it was a fairly grainy film. In bright sunny weather I sometimes used Ilford FP3 film or Pan F, much less grainy films but needing plenty of light as they were not as fast as the HP3.

With this first year under my belt, the next birthday was soon approaching and I announced that I would like 'a better camera, please' for my fourteenth – John Edgington was right, the Perkeo had challenged me and I now wanted to take things to a new level. Having spent a lot of time in the local camera shop in Hatch End – to where we had moved in early 1963 – I had done a fair amount of research and decided that I needed what was known as a 'rangefinder miniature' – a 35mm camera with coupled rangefinder for accurate focusing. The Leica was the top of the range for this sort of camera, but I knew such a thing was out of the question and I set my heart on another Voigtländer, this time the Vito CLR model.

The going rate for this camera was around £54, at which my father baulked (to put this in context, the house that we had moved into in Harrow Weald cost about £750, albeit several years earlier). By this time, however, he had moved on to a somewhat better job with Taylor Woodrow and discovered that their 'buying department' could purchase items for management members at a discounted rate – 33% for something like this, which brought the price down to £36. So the purchase went ahead and I got my new camera – with a proviso. The maximum my father could run to for a present was £12 (he did have three other children's birthdays to consider as well!) and so it was announced that I would have to pay back the remaining £24 as a loan. It was a hard bargain but a lesson learned – not everything you want is going to fall into your hands. The main thing was, of course, that I had the camera – it had a 50mm f2.8 Color-Skopar lens and Pronto-LK shutter with speeds from 1/15 to 1/500 second and bulb (time) exposure, coupled rangefinder and exposure meter, together with combined lever wind and shutter tensioning – a very sophisticated tool for a fourteen-year-old.

I did use a couple of cassettes of 35mm black and white film to start with this camera, but almost immediately progressed to using colour reversal film for slides, initially Kodak Ektachrome at 32asa. This film could be bought without the processing costs included – it was possible to process it yourself if you had the facilities, which I didn't – so although it was cheaper to buy, the processing cost had to be added afterwards. It was also less costly to get it processed unmounted and then mount the slides yourself – this was something I could do, of course.

Even so, the costs were high and film had to be eked out carefully with every shot counting – none of the rapid-fire that takes place nowadays with digital cameras.

Many of the 'old school' of photographers would only take shots in bright sunshine and this, of course, was the ideal. By this time though that was not really an option as if you were to go out only on sunny days, your subject matter may well have been scrapped in the meantime.

The speed of colour film was generally very low in comparison to what was available in monochrome, and it was vitally important that your film could cope with low light levels. Because of this, I soon changed to Agfa CT18 film (18 DIN – 50asa), which gave me an extra half-a-stop over Ektachrome and a whole stop over Kodachrome 1 at 25asa. The downside was that the Agfa film was somewhat softer and grainier than either of the Kodak films, though it was process paid and came back in decent quality mounts!

It did mean, though, that I could get shots in poor light that I would not have been able to get with the slower films – so better a slightly grainy shot than no shot at all!

I did experiment with a couple of rolls of Gevacolor film; this was the same speed as Agfa CT18, was slightly sharper, a bit less grainy and gave a good colour rendition, but I decided to stick with Agfa – just as well as the Gevacolor shots have faded very badly over the years. Agfa CT18 is also not noted for being a good 'archive' film, but I have been lucky and most of my slides are still as good as new – surprisingly perhaps, some of my Ektachrome slides have not survived so well.

Nowadays, with the wonders of computer processing, many faults of fading, ageing etc. can be corrected as film is scanned and really brought back to life again, looking as they originally did – even including the Gevacolor.

So my first colour shot on the new Vito CLR was of newly restored LNER A3 No. 4472 *Flying Scotsman* on its inaugural run in preservation at London Paddington station with the 'Festiniog Railway Society' special to Minffordd and Porthmadog, which it worked as far as Ruabon in April 1963, in appalling weather.

Our visits and trips continued. Sometimes we would be on railtours at opposite ends of the country on subsequent days – what a blessing that my father was such an enthusiast as I would never have managed to get as much travelling done under my own resources. Nevertheless, a lot of travelling was done by bicycle, such as trips to Willesden, Old Oak Common and Southall sheds, Bushey Water Troughs, Hadley Wood and so on.

As soon as I was old enough to get a provisional licence to ride a motorbike, I was able to borrow my sister's Honda 50 – hardly a racing machine but it meant I could get further afield, and as my competence increased I graduated to larger and faster bikes to get me to even more distant locations.

Considering all the limitations, I was able to get many shots from around much of the country, though I was unfortunately not able to do much in Scotland, apart from a few railtours. I had been on a couple of RCTS shed bashes to Scotland in 1957, and again in 1960, and saw some wonderful survivors from years before; sadly though, this was before I had a camera.

I do have plenty of memories of lines and locos long gone before I started my photography and have been able to fill many gaps in my own efforts with purchases of original slides from older photographers, most of whom have now passed on but have left a lasting legacy. These include D.E. 'Doug' White, Mike Burnett, Major E.A.S. Cotton (AKA 'Peter') and T.J. 'John' Edgington, all of whom I knew as friends of my father. There are also some photos by unknown photographers; these photos were purchased years ago from Mike Higson of 'The Roundhouse' fame.

The vast majority of pictures you will see in this book are my own work, interspersed with older shots from my collection, which are captioned as such, and I hope you will find them all enjoyable.

The majority of photographs are taken along the lines from Waterloo to Bournemouth as this became the last mainstay of steam workings – the lines in Kent had succumbed to electrification by the early 1960s and I recall seeing many displaced locos from this area stored prior to scrapping, though again, before my days of photography.

The photos start at Waterloo station, which became the last stronghold of steam in the London area after the end of the few remaining steam services into Marylebone in September 1966, and spread out around some London suburbs, then into Kent and Sussex before heading further south west along the Bournemouth line, taking in the Isle of Wight. The time I had available, not to mention the lack of funds, meant that sadly I was not able to cover the lines in Devon and Cornwall, these succumbing to being run-down shadows of previous times or fairly early closure.

Where possible, I have included comprehensive captions to the photos to give loco and/or location backgrounds: these give some build dates, allocations throughout the career of the locos, withdrawal, storage and scrapping notes. Please note that these are generalised rather than specific details that have been taken from the usual sources (i.e. not primary sources), such as the RCTS's *The Railway Observer*, SLS Journals, Peter Hands' booklets on *What Happened to Steam*, Jeffery Grayer's *Scrapping the Southern* etc. Much of this information compiled into a major database by Peter Kellett, to whom I am very grateful. In recent years, due to a great deal of work done by the HSBT Project (What Really Happened to Steam – **www.whatreallyhappenedtosteam.co.uk**), it has come to light that much of the information used by many authors is incorrect, apparently due to the activities of one 'rogue' reporter. Thus the information given here should not be taken as Gospel, though I have attempted to use the latest available details, but as the HSBT Project is ongoing, further discrepancies between published data and actual events may come to light.

Glossary of Terms

AD	Army Department (with reference to 'Austerity' Locomotives)		LMS	London Midland & Scottish Railway
			LNER	London North Eastern Railway
AKA	Also Known As		LNWR	London & North Western Railway
BR	British Railways		LSWR	London & South Western Railway
BR(S)	British Railways (Southern Region)		MPD	Motive Power Depot
BRCW	Birmingham Railway Carriage & Wagon Company		NER	North Eastern Region (of BR)
DC	Direct Current		NX	Entrance – Exit (with reference to signalling consoles/panels)
DE	Diesel Electric		PS	Paddle Steamer
DN&S	Didcot, Newbury & Southampton		RCTS	Railway Correspondence & Travel Society
ECML	East Coast Main Line		RO	Railway Observer – Journal of the RCTS
ECS	Empty Coaching Stock		ROD	Railway Operating Division (Royal Engineers)
EMU	Electric Multiple Unit		S&DJR	Somerset & Dorset Joint Railway
EPB	Electro-Pneumatic Brake (with reference to EMUs)		SECR	South Eastern & Chatham Railway
GWR	Great Western Railway		SER	South Eastern Railway
IoW	Isle of Wight		SLS	Stephenson Locomotive Society
JP	Justice of the Peace		SR	Southern Railway
KESR	Kent & East Sussex Railway		TOPS	Total Operations Processing System (a computerised system of locomotive and rolling stock management)
LBSCR	London Brighton & South Coast Railway			
LCDR	London Chatham & Dover Railway		USATC	United States Army Transportation Corps
LCGB	Locomotive Club of Great Britain		WCML	West Coast Main Line
LMR	Longmoor Military Railway (or London Midland Region of BR)		WD	War Department (with reference to 'Austerity' Locomotives)

LSWR Beattie 0298 Class 'Well Tanks' 2-4-0WTs Nos. 30585 and 30587 are at the head of the joint RCTS/SLS 'South Western Suburban' Railtour before departure from Waterloo station on Sunday 2 December 1962. This tour was so popular that a repeat was run two weeks later, after which the engines were withdrawn from service, though happily, both survived.

These locos were two of the three survivors of a class of eighty-five engines built between 1863 and 1875, mostly by Beyer, Peacock & Company, for use on LSWR suburban services. Later displaced by larger engines they were transferred to depots outside London and thirty-one were converted to tender engines. Six were rebuilt into the form seen here but the entire class had been withdrawn by 1899 except for the three which ended up at Wadebridge in 1895 to work the china clay branch to Wenfordbridge, with its severe curvature. No. 30585 was originally LSWR No. 314, Beyer, Peacock No. 1414 of June 1874, and 30587 was No. 298, Beyer, Peacock No. 1412 of May 1874 – long lived engines indeed!

Seen from the departing RCTS/SLS joint 'South Western Suburban' Railtour, rebuilt Bulleid 'Merchant Navy' Class 4-6-2 No. 35026 *Lamport & Holt Line* makes a simultaneous departure with a down west of England express at 11:00. Also leaving is a down suburban EMU with photographers hanging out of the windows, hoping to overtake both the Pacific and the tour train hauled by Beattie 'Well Tanks' Nos. 30585 and 30587.

This departure was on Sunday 16 December 1962 – a repeat of the tour run two weeks earlier. No. 35026 was built at Eastleigh Works in December 1948 and rebuilt without the air-smoothed casing and with Walschaerts valve-gear in January 1957, also at Eastleigh. At this time in its career it was allocated to 72A, Exmouth Junction MPD. It was withdrawn from service in March 1967 from Weymouth shed and after being stored there for a few months it was scrapped at Cashmore's, Newport, in September 1967.

Bulleid 'Austerity'Q1 Class 0-6-0 No. 33027 has a full head of steam as it waits at Waterloo station on Sunday 22 March 1964 for a 09:00 departure in charge of the joint RCTS/LCGB 'The Sussex Downsman' Railtour. This engine worked the first leg of the tour as far as Horsham.

Q1s were not common sights at Waterloo as they were normally freight engines, built during the Second World War to cater for wartime extra traffic. They were the last 0-6-0 type built in the country, and the most powerful, being designated power class 5F by BR. Forty engines were built in 1942, the first twenty at Brighton Works and the second twenty at Ashford Works.

No. 33027 was allocated to Feltham (70B) MPD at the time of the photo and was withdrawn from service in January 1966, by that time allocated to Guildford. After storage at Guildford, Eastleigh, and Severn Tunnel Junction, it reached Buttigieg's, Newport, in August 1966 and was scrapped there the following month. The first member of the class, No. 33001, is preserved as part of the National Collection.

A couple of spotters watch proceedings at the end of the platform at Waterloo station as BR Standard 3MT 2-6-2T No. 82010 prepares to depart with ECS to the sidings at Clapham Junction on Saturday 24 April 1965. The engine was designed and built in June 1952 at Swindon Works, as one of a class of forty-five locos, and was allocated to the Southern Region all its life, initially at Exmouth Junction MPD. It was withdrawn from service from Nine Elms shed soon after this photo was taken, and after a short storage period at Nine Elms and Severn Tunnel Junction, was scrapped by Bird's at Morriston, Swansea in October 1965. None of the class made it into preservation, but at the time of writing, a new-build loco, No. 82045, is in the course of construction.

British Railways Standard 4MT 2-6-4T No. 80154 (the last engine to be built at Brighton Works) brings the ECS for the 'Bournemouth Belle' Pullman train into Waterloo station on Saturday 24 April 1965. The coaches are all Pullmans, apart from the first, which is a BR Mk.1 in Western Region livery and is being used as a luggage van. This train departed for Southampton and Bournemouth at 12:30, usually with a 'Merchant Navy' Pacific at the head.

No. 80154 was the last of the 155 strong class, designed at Brighton and built at Brighton, Derby and Doncaster from 1951 until 1957. It initially entered service allocated to Brighton and was withdrawn from Nine Elms shed in April 1967, after just ten years. It was scrapped by Buttigieg's, Newport in October 1967, after storage at Nine Elms and Salisbury.

U Class 2-6-0s Nos. 31791 and 31639 are at the head of the RCTS 'The Longmoor Rail Tour' at Waterloo station on Saturday 30 April 1966. They worked the train as far as Woking where LMR WD 'Austerity' 2-10-0 No. AD 600 *Gordon* took over for the run to Liss and onto the Longmoor system.

This tour was a repeat, due to very high demand, of the train run two weeks earlier, when this leg was worked by N Class 2-6-0 No. 31411 together with 31639 in very dull weather. In the meantime, 31411 had been withdrawn from service so was replaced by 31791.

U Class 2-6-0s Nos. 31791 and 31639 (out of picture) are at the head of the RCTS 'The Longmoor Rail Tour' at Waterloo station on Saturday 30 April 1966. In the background is the 'new' signal box opened on 18 October 1936, a one-off design and the largest constructed by the SR, as part of the scheme to control the line out to Hampton Court Junction with four aspect colour-light signalling. It had a Westinghouse Brake & Signal Co. style 'L' power lever frame in three sections with a total of 309 levers. It replaced three older mechanical signal boxes at Waterloo – 'A', 'B' and 'C' – and also Vauxhall East and West signal boxes. A new NX Panel replaced the original panels in 1984, still in the same building, but this was moved to a temporary box during construction of the International Eurostar terminal. The signal box closed on 30 October 1990 for demolition, and control of the station was later passed to Wimbledon Signalling Centre from 21 April 1991.

BR Standard 5MT 4-6-0 No. 73018 arrives at Waterloo station with an up express from Salisbury on the morning of Saturday 30 April 1966, as an EMU departs from the station. No. 73018 was built at Derby Works, entering service from the end of September 1951 and allocated to Nottingham MPD. It transferred to the Western Region based at Shrewsbury from September 1953 and then moved on to become a Swindon loco from the end of 1956.

Transferred again from September 1958, this time to the Southern Region with Weymouth as its home shed, it ended up at Guildford in early 1967. Withdrawal from service came with the end of steam on the Southern Region in July 1967, when the loco went back to Weymouth for storage until December 1967. The final move came in January 1968, to Cashmore's, Newport, where it was scrapped the same month.

Southern Railway U class 2-6-0s Nos. 31791 and 31639 stand at the bufferstops at platform 14 at Waterloo station on Saturday 30 April 1966, having arrived with the final leg from Windsor & Eton Riverside of the RCTS 'The Longmoor Rail Tour'. This was the second running of the tour.

No. 31791 was originally designed by Richard Maunsell and built as SECR 'River' Class K 2-6-4T No. A791 *River Adur* in May 1925 by Armstrong Whitworth. The twenty locos in the class (plus one more three cylinder loco classified K1) were not very stable engines and after No. A800 *River Cray* was involved in the Sevenoaks accident in August 1927, all the class was rebuilt as U 2-6-0s, plus one U1, losing

their names in the process.

A791 was rebuilt at Eastleigh Works in May 1928, and renumbered 1791. At nationalisation in 1948, it was allocated to Yeovil Town shed and gained its BR number 31791 in March 1949. Around September 1958 the loco moved on to Exmouth Junction until June 1959 before returning to Yeovil Town, moving again to Eastleigh from March 1960. Its final reallocation was to Guildford from December 1963 from where it was withdrawn on 5 June 1966. After a short period in store at Eastleigh until August 1966, it was eventually scrapped at Cashmore's, Newport, in September 1966.

Southern Railway U class 2-6-0s Nos. 31791 and 31639 stand at the bufferstops in platform 14 at Waterloo station, having arrived with the final leg from Windsor & Eton Riverside of the RCTS 'The Longmoor Rail Tour'. This was the second running of the tour on Saturday 30 April 1966.

No. 31639 was built at Ashford Works in May 1931 as Class U No. 1639, with detail differences from the original batch rebuilt from 'River' Class K 2-6-4Ts; the class eventually numbered fifty engines. Allocated to Faversham at nationalisation (from 1 January 1948), the loco gained its BR number 31639 in December 1948.

After spending the 1950s and early 1960s moving between Salisbury, Yeovil Town and Eastleigh depots, as well as Bournemouth, Hither Green and Norwood Junction, the engine ended up at Guildford shed from December 1963, where it remained until withdrawal on 5 June 1966. These two engines – Nos. 31639 and 31791 – were the last survivors of the class. Stored at Guildford and Eastleigh until August 1966, No. 31639 met its end at Cashmore's, Newport, in September 1966.

Rebuilt Bulleid 'West Country' Class 4-6-2 No. 34108 *Wincanton* had arrived at Waterloo station a short while earlier with an up express from Bournemouth, on Tuesday 28 March 1967. While it waits to return to Nine Elms depot, the driver exchanges a glance with a photographer walking along the adjacent platform.

No. 34108 was built at Brighton Works and entered service in April 1950 from Bournemouth shed, where it remained until February 1958.

It was reallocated to Exmouth Junction until April 1961, then going to Eastleigh Works for rebuilding, returning to Exmouth Junction once complete. Transferred to Salisbury shed in November 1963, it remained there until withdrawn in June 1967, and was stored until September 1967. Further storage was at Dock Street Goods Yard, Newport, from October 1967 until September 1968, then at J. Buttigieg's at Newport, where it was scrapped during November 1968.

Bulleid rebuilt 'West Country' Class 4-6-2 No. 34004 *Yeovil* is at the head of the prestigious 'Bournemouth Belle' Pullman train, the 12:30 departure from Waterloo, as it approaches Vauxhall station soon after setting off on Friday 1 July 1966. The engine is at least still carrying its nameplates, though it is filthy dirty!

The loco was built at Brighton Works and entered service as SR No. 21C104 in June 1945; it was named *Yeovil* on 2 November 1945. At the time of nationalisation it was based at Exmouth Junction shed and remained there until January 1958 when it went for rebuilding to Eastleigh Works. Once rebuilding was complete, it was allocated to Bricklayers Arms at the end of February 1958, moving on again to Stewarts Lane from February 1961 and then to Eastleigh from May 1961. Its final reallocation was to Bournemouth in October 1965, remaining there until its withdrawal in July 1967 at the end of steam. It was moved into store at Weymouth shed until December 1967, finally being broken up at Cashmore's, Newport later the same month.

Apart from seeing trains on their way in and out of Waterloo, Vauxhall station also saw light engine moves to and from Nine Elms shed, as well as ECS workings to and from the sidings at Clapham Junction. For some years, the platform on the western side of the station was fitted out with equipment for emptying milk tank wagons, and these trains were regular visitors. Here, on Friday 1 July 1966, rebuilt Bulleid 'West Country' Class 4-6-2 No. 34101 *Hartland* runs tenderfirst light engine through Vauxhall station as it makes its way to Nine Elms MPD for servicing after arriving at Waterloo with an express earlier in the day.

No. 34101 was built at Eastleigh Works in February 1950, entering service from March of that year at Stewarts Lane MPD, which remained its home base for the next ten years, then moving back to Eastleigh for rebuilding during September 1960. After rebuilding, the engine returned to Stewarts Lane for a short period before moving on to Bricklayers Arms from May 1961, then to Brighton from June 1962, transferring to Nine Elms from June 1963. It was reallocated a final time to Eastleigh around September 1964 and eventually withdrawn from there in July 1966. Stored until October 1966 at Eastleigh it was sold to Woodham's and moved to Barry, South Wales, ostensibly for scrap. There, with many others, it languished until resold in July 1978 for preservation and has since been restored to working order at the North Yorkshire Moors Railway.

Unrebuilt Bulleid 'West Country' Class 4-6-2 No. 34002 *Salisbury* is looking very clean for this period, when most engines were filthy. On Sunday 3 July 1966, a gloriously sunny day, it is backing down light engine from Nine Elms MPD to Waterloo, having just passed Vauxhall station. It had been cleaned up to work a special train that should have been hauled by Gresley LNER V2 Class 2-6-2 No. 60919, which had reached Nine Elms but was declared a failure and unable to work the tour!

No. 34002 was built at Brighton Works and entered service as 21C102 in June 1945, being named on 11 July 1945 at Salisbury by the Mayor, Councillor A. Courtney. It became No. 34002 in October 1948 after nationalisation and spent the majority of its working life based at Exmouth Junction MPD. Its first transfer was to Eastleigh during August/September 1964 but this was short-lived, the engine moving again to Nine Elms from January 1965. It was withdrawn in April 1967 and stored at Nine Elms until August, before reaching Cashmore's, Newport, in October 1967, to be scrapped the same month.

BR Standard 5MT 4-6-0 No. 73022 approaches Vauxhall station alongside an EMU whilst in charge of the 09:50 excursion train from Waterloo to Southampton Terminus, carrying the headcode 'SPL 3', on the morning of Sunday 3 July 1966. No. 73022 was built by BR at Derby Works in October 1951 and originally allocated to Chester (LMR, Code 6A) shed, before being transferred to several Western Region depots. By mid-1964 it had arrived on the Southern Region at Eastleigh shed and was later transferred to Guildford before ending up at Nine Elms. It was withdrawn in April 1967 and after a period in store at Salisbury was scrapped at Cashmore's, Newport, during November 1967.

Unrebuilt Bulleid 'West Country' Class 4-6-2 No. 34002 *Salisbury* has been nicely cleaned up to work this special train, the 09:52 LCGB 'The Green Arrow Railtour' from Waterloo, here approaching Vauxhall on Sunday 3 July 1966. No. 34002 was standing in for LNER Gresley V2 ('Green Arrow' Class) 2-6-2 No. 60919 which was due to work the train.

No. 60919 had arrived from Dundee at Nine Elms MPD, but was failed on the day, so 34002 substituted. No. 34002 worked the outward train as far as Salisbury and the return run from Weymouth (double-headed together with LMS 'Black 5' 4-6-0 No. 45493 as far as Bournemouth Central) to Waterloo, booked to arrive at 19:55.

From the Geoff Plumb Collection of original slides, photo by D.E. White. Southern Railway V Class 'Schools' 4-4-0 No. 30927 *Clifton* sits amongst the detritus in the yard at Nine Elms MPD between duties on Sunday 7 May 1961. The shed remained open until the end of steam on the Southern Region on Sunday 9 July 1967 and closed completely on 31 October 1967, although the last dumped locos remained until December 1967. The depot tracks were lifted during January and February 1968 and the remnants of the site demolished during September and October 1968.

The 'Schools' Class was designed by R.E.L. Maunsell and forty engines were built at Eastleigh Works from 1930 to 1935, becoming the most powerful 4-4-0 locos in the country and all named after English public schools. From 1938, Bulleid modified twenty-one of the engines with Lemaître multiple blast-pipes and large diameter chimneys, totally altering their appearance, though 30927 retained its original single blast-pipe and chimney. No. 30927 spent most of its BR existence based at Dover and then Bricklayers Arms depots, followed by a very short spell at Feltham during 1961. Its final allocation was to Nine Elms from March 1961 and it was withdrawn in January 1962. Moved back to Eastleigh by February 1962, it was scrapped there the following month.

Almost lost in the extensive layout of Nine Elms MPD, BR Standard 3MT 2-6-2T No. 82006 simmers between station pilot and ECS duties on Sunday 3 July 1966. The engine was formerly allocated to the Western Region, where it had been repainted in plain green livery at its final overhaul, by now somewhat soiled! Built at Swindon Works in May 1952, 82006 had been a Machynlleth engine since mid-1961 and was transferred to Nine Elms during 1965. It was withdrawn in September 1966 and scrapped at Buttigieg's, Newport, during February 1967.

BR Standard 5MT 4-6-0 No. 73029 sits at Nine Elms depot between duties, on Sunday 3 July 1966. In front of it is rebuilt 'West Country' 4-6-2 No. 34101 *Hartland*. The chimneys of Battersea Power Station can just be seen above the shed roof.

No. 73029 was built at BR Derby Works in June 1953 and was initially allocated to Blackpool MPD. With various moves between depots under its belt it had recently been transferred to Nine Elms from Guildford. Withdrawn from Nine Elms in July 1967, it spent a period in store at Salisbury, making its final journey in March 1968 to Cashmore's, Newport, for scrapping.

Two BR Standard Tanks stand rather forlornly at Nine Elms MPD on Sunday 3 July 1966. Nearer to camera is 3MT 2-6-2T No. 82026, which looks as though it might still be in occasional use, while further from camera 4MT 2-6-4T No. 80144 looks out of use. Quite what was put in the water supply at Nine Elms I don't know, but it certainly played havoc with the paintwork on tanksides! Two of the chimneys of Battersea Power Station can be seen above the shed roof.

No. 82026 was built at Swindon Works in November 1954 and originally went to the North Eastern Region, based at Kirkby Stephen MPD. It moved several times whilst on the NER, first to Darlington, then Scarborough, Low Moor and Copley Hill before being transferred to the Southern Region at Guildford from September 1963. Further moves saw it at Bournemouth and, finally, Nine Elms from September 1964. It had been withdrawn on 26 June 1966, just before this photo was taken – it was stored here until September 1966 then taken to Buttigieg's, Newport, and scrapped in October 1966.

Rebuilt Bulleid 'Merchant Navy' Class 4-6-2 No. 35028 *Clan Line* simmers between duties at Nine Elms MPD on Sunday 3 July 1966. No. 35028 was built at Eastleigh Works in December 1948 and was allocated to Bournemouth, followed by Dover and Stewarts Lane depots. Nine Elms became its home from June 1959 and it returned there after a rebuild at Eastleigh Works in October 1959.

No. 35028 was a Weymouth engine from early 1964 until the first part of 1967 when it was transferred to Nine Elms. It was withdrawn at the end of Southern Region steam in July 1967 and was sold straight into preservation to the Merchant Navy Locomotive Preservation Society on 13 August 1967. Initially housed at Longmoor and then at Ashford, the engine became a regular performer on the main line ever since, apart from during the infamous 'steam ban' years (from August 1968 until October 1971) and overhauls. Its first main line tour in preservation was on 27 April 1974, where it ran from Basingstoke to Westbury.

In the last of the afternoon sunshine, BR Standard 5MT 4-6-0 No. 73088 *Joyous Gard* approaches Earlsfield station with a down express from Waterloo to Bournemouth on Friday 23 December 1966. The loco was built at BR Derby Works in September 1955 and, apart from a short spell at Oxford shed in February 1956, spent all of its short life on the Southern Region, initially allocated to Stewarts Lane. It was a Nine Elms engine for the majority of its service but was transferred to Guildford towards the end of 1965 and was withdrawn in October 1966 and stored at Eastleigh – so was it returned to service for extra Christmas traffic?

By May 1967 it was at Salisbury and then moved to Cashmore's, Newport, where it was scrapped in June 1967. The engine was one of the twenty which took the names from withdrawn Urie N15 Class 'King Arthur' 4-6-0s during 1959, becoming known as 'Standard Arthurs'. No sign of hi-visibility clothing amongst the track gang!

From the Geoff Plumb Collection of original slides, photographer not known, but possibly E.A.S. Cotton. Maunsell SR 0-6-0DE No. 15202, one of three built at Ashford Works in 1937, does some shunting during March 1963 at Hither Green, then its home depot. The locos were generally based at Norwood Yard but did undertake the odd trip workings. Similar locos were designed by Bulleid after the Second World War, the forerunners of the ubiquitous Class 08 shunters. These three survived until around November 1964 and all were eventually scrapped, this one by Cashmore's, Newport in November 1966.

From the Geoff Plumb Collection of original slides, photographer not known, but possibly E.A.S. Cotton. Southern Railway Maunsell Class N 2-6-0 No. 31410 on shed at Norwood Junction in March 1963, looking in quite good external condition. Its SR style chimney has been replaced with a BR Standard type and it appears to have 'home made' extensions to the tops of its smoke deflector plates. Behind are a Class Q 0-6-0 and another 'Mogul', whilst a couple of spotters disappear into the murk of the shed.

Built at Ashford Works in November 1933, at the date of the picture 31410 was a Stewarts Lane engine but was transferred to Norwood Junction during June/July 1963 and then to Redhill from August/September 1963. Its final transfer was to Guildford at the end of 1963 and its withdrawal followed in November 1964. Following storage at Guildford and Eastleigh, it met its end at Bird's, Morriston, Swansea, in March 1965.

Seen from the RCTS/SLS Joint 'South Western Suburban' Railtour tour train on Sunday 2 December 1962 as it returned from Chessington South, Beattie 0298 Class 2-4-0WTs Nos. 30585 and 30587 are making their way to Wimbledon Yard, passing Wimbledon 'C' Signal Box, to take over the train once again for the remainder of the journey. The tour ran again two weeks later due to popular demand, after which the three surviving 'Well Tanks' were withdrawn, though these two made it into preservation.

Seen from the tour train on Sunday 16 December 1962, Urie Class H16 4-6-2T No. 30517 is running light engine alongside the goods yard at Wimbledon in order to be in position to take over the RCTS/SLS Joint 'South Western Suburban' Railtour from the two Beattie 'Well Tanks' after their return from Hampton Court. The train reversed direction here, with the H16 working to Chessington South then back to Wimbledon for the 2-4-0WTs to take over again. An unidentified SR 2-6-0 can also just be seen at the head of a freight train in the yard.

No. 30517 was one of five built in 1921 and mainly used for shunting in the yard at Feltham and also for trip workings of freight around London, and was allocated to Feltham shed for much of its career. It was withdrawn soon after working these tours in December 1962 and was stored at Feltham and then Eastleigh for a short time before being scrapped there in June 1963.

BR(S) 4EPB Suburban set DC EMU No. 5229 approaches Wimbledon station on the line from Streatham on a sunny afternoon in February 1971. The headcode 06 would indicate an ECS working to Strawberry Hill Depot. The 4EPBs were an SR design built between 1951 and 1957 and subsequently became Class 415/1, the sets numbered from 5001 to 5260 and allocated to Slade Green depot. The final units in the series lasted until 1995.

On an unspecified day in February 1971, an unidentified member of the ten-strong Class 74 DC Electro-Diesel locos, rebuilt from the earlier Class 71 series locos (Pre-TOPS Type HA, built from 1958 to 1960 at Doncaster Works), passes the 'A' Signal Box at Wimbledon with a southbound express carrying the code 91. This was presumably a fast working from Waterloo to Weymouth, though the loco would probably be replaced at Bournemouth (by a Class 33 diesel) as the 74s were pretty unreliable on diesel power.

The ten members of the Class were rebuilt from Class 71 at Crewe Works from November 1967 to May 1968 and were renumbered from their original E5xxx numbers to E6101–10, though not in sequence. Pre-TOPS they were Type HB and under TOPS they were renumbered again as Class 74001–74010 from the end of 1973. No. 74006, formerly E5023, was the first to be withdrawn from service in June 1976; all had gone by December 1977.

Wimbledon 'A' Signal Box was one of the SR's Art Deco 'Streamline Moderne' (known as 'Odeon-style') structures introduced from around 1936, though this one was built in 1948. Similar style boxes at Woking and Horsham are listed by Historic England as 'Type SR 13' boxes, and Wimbledon 'A' has now joined them.

Unrebuilt Bulleid 'West Country' Class 4-6-2 No. 34015 *Exmouth* races its up Bournemouth express through Raynes Park en route for Waterloo in somewhat stormy-looking weather on Tuesday 28 March 1967. The engine is in reasonable external condition, but has already had its nameplates removed.

The loco was built at Brighton Works and entered service as 21C115 in November 1945, and was allocated, appropriately, to Exmouth Junction shed. It was named at Exmouth by the town's Mayor,

Councillor J. Down, on 26 June 1946 and was renumbered 34015 in April 1948 after nationalisation. Apart from a short period in store at Salisbury during the winter of 1950/51 it remained at Exmouth Junction until re-allocation to Salisbury in September 1964. It was withdrawn from Salisbury in April 1967 and was then stored at Nine Elms until August 1967, finally being scrapped at Cashmore's, Newport, during September 1967.

Unrebuilt Bulleid 'West Country' Class light Pacific No. 34015 *Exmouth* races its up Bournemouth express through Raynes Park bound for Waterloo in somewhat stormy-looking weather on Tuesday 28 March 1967. The engine is in fairly clean condition for this period, but has already had its nameplates removed.

Raynes Park station was opened on 30 October 1871 with through fast lines and staggered platforms on the slow lines, with a long, angled footbridge over the lines to reach the up platform. The station is also the non-conflicting junction between the main line and the lines to Epsom and Chessington South.

LSWR Urie H16 Class 6F 4-6-2T No. 30517 is running round the stock of the RCTS/SLS Joint 'South Western Suburban' Railtour at Chessington South station on the afternoon of Sunday 2 December 1962. It had taken over the train from the Beattie 'Well Tanks' at Wimbledon Yard and they took over once again on the return to Wimbledon.

This loco was one of five built to Urie's design at Eastleigh Works in 1921 for heavy freight trip working and all were allocated to Feltham MPD (70B). The other four engines had all been withdrawn in November 1962, then 30517 was taken out of service on 29 December 1962 and stored at Feltham until January 1963. Further storage followed at Eastleigh and it was eventually scrapped there in June 1963.

Southern Railway Bulleid Q1 Class 0-6-0 No. 33012 approaches Berrylands station with a down local freight trip, possibly to Feltham Yard via Chertsey and Staines, on Wednesday 8 April 1964. The loco was built at Brighton Works in September 1942 and numbered C12. At nationalisation it was a Guildford engine and subsequently transferred to Feltham in March 1948; it was renumbered 33012 in January 1950. It remained a Feltham engine until September 1964 when it moved back to Guildford, though only for a short time as it was withdrawn in November 1964.

Stored at Guildford until January 1965, it moved on to Eastleigh during February and finally to Bird's, Morriston, Swansea, where it was cut up during May 1965. Parts of the sewage works at Hogsmill and Berrylands can be seen to the left of the picture – both these were served by small internal systems 2ft 0in gauge railways at one time. Lower Marsh Lane, which runs between the two and passes under the bridge in the picture, was deemed to be one of the smelliest places in the London area!

LSWR Beattie 0298 Class 'Well Tanks' 2-4-0WTs Nos. 30585 and 30587 are at the head of the joint RCTS/SLS 'South Western Suburban' Railtour at Surbiton station on Sunday 16 December 1962. This tour was so popular that this was a repeat of a run two weeks earlier, after which the engines were withdrawn from service, though happily, both survived. They are standing at Platform 4 adjacent to the goods yard, then still in use, but nowadays, like so many others, the station car park. At the end of this tour, after dark at Waterloo station, the two locos returned light engine to Nine Elms shed and I was lucky enough to ride on the footplate of 30585 for the trip – too dark for photos though…

Southern Railway rebuilt Bulleid 'Battle of Britain' Class 4-6-2 No. 34050 *Royal Observer Corps* looks quite spick & span as it approaches Surbiton station with a down west of England express from Waterloo, on Wednesday 8 April 1964. As well as the nameplate and associated badge, this engine also carried the colours on the cabside below the number.

No. 34050 was built by the Southern Railway at Brighton Works and entered service in December 1946 as 21C150, renumbered to 34050 after nationalisation. Its first allocation was to Salisbury depot with

short spells at Nine Elms and Exmouth Junction, returning to Salisbury in mid-1951 until August 1958 when it was rebuilt at Eastleigh and took up residence afterwards back at Salisbury until late 1960. It then spent a year or so at Bricklayers Arms before migrating again to Nine Elms from 1961 to 1964, from where it was working on this occasion. Later in 1964 its final move was to Eastleigh depot from where it was withdrawn in August 1965. After storage at Eastleigh until November 1965 it was scrapped at Bird's, Morriston, Swansea, during December 1965.

A couple of track workers, not exactly highly visible, cross the lines on the left and a fellow photographer captures the progress of rebuilt Bulleid 'West Country' Class 4-6-2 No. 34095 *Brentor* as it approaches the platforms at Surbiton station with an up west of England express to Waterloo on Wednesday 8 April 1964. The days of being able to stand at the bottom of platform ramps and open barrow-crossings are long gone!

No. 34095 was built at Eastleigh in October 1949 and rebuilt in January 1961, and was one of the locos that did not carry a coat of arms together with its nameplate. No. 34095 was initially a Bournemouth engine until early 1956 when it was transferred to Nine Elms and returned there after rebuilding. Later in 1964 it was moved to Eastleigh shed from where it was withdrawn in July 1967. It was stored at Weymouth until January 1968 before ending up at Cashmore's, Newport, where it was scrapped during April 1968.The signal box was the first of the Southern 'Streamline Moderne' Art Deco Type 13, built in 1936, other examples being at Woking and Wimbledon.

BR Standard 5MT Class 4-6-0 No. 73083 *Pendragon* rushes through Surbiton station on the down fast line with a semi-fast working from Waterloo to Basingstoke, on Wednesday 8 April 1964. No. 73083 was built by BR at Derby Works in July 1955 and initially allocated to Stewarts Lane; it remained a Southern Region loco for all its short twelve year life.

Transferred to Nine Elms during the period from 2 May 1959 to 14 June 1959, it remained there until transferred again to Feltham depot during August/September 1964, so was a Nine Elms engine at the time of this photo. It was stored at Feltham until transferred again to Weymouth during October/November 1964 and was eventually withdrawn from there in September 1966. It met its fate at Cashmore's, Newport, in February 1967, after further storage at Nine Elms.

In the gathering gloom of a winter's afternoon, Beattie 0298 Class 2-4-0WT 'Well Tanks' Nos. 30585 and 30587 run round the tour train at Shepperton, terminus of the branch from Strawberry Hill and Teddington. This was during the first run of the joint RCTS/SLS 'South Western Suburban' Railtour on Sunday 2 December 1962; it was repeated two weeks later by popular demand and I was able to travel on it again!

LSWR 0298 Class Beattie 2-4-0WTs Nos. 30585 and 30587 are in charge of the joint RCTS/SLS 'South Western Suburban' Railtour on Sunday 2 December 1962 and have now reached the terminus of the branch to Hampton Court where they were due to take water before running round the train. Despite it being a sunny day it was very cold and the water supply was frozen solid. With their small water tanks almost empty this was something of a crisis and preparations were made to drop the fires – fortunately, someone contacted the local Fire Brigade who turned up in time to replenish the engines' tanks.

Having taken water at Hampton Court station, Beattie 2-4-0WTs Nos. 30585 and 30587 are running round the stock of the joint RCTS/SLS 'South Western Suburban' Railtour prior to retracing their steps to Wimbledon, where 30517 took over for the trip to Chessington South.

This was during the second running of the tour on Sunday 16 December 1962 – no mishaps with the water supply this time! The locos were coupled bunker to bunker for the second tour.

Maunsell S15 Class 4-6-0 No. 30837 was out of steam and the sole occupant of the running shed at Feltham Yard on Sunday 13 June 1965. This class was a development of Urie's earlier Class S15, introduced in 1920 as a mixed traffic variant of the N15 'King Arthur' Class and introduced in 1927.

No. 30837 was one of the members of the class fitted with a six-wheel tender for working on the Central Section of the SR. Built at Eastleigh Works in January 1928 as No. 837, the loco was renumbered 30837 after nationalisation, at which point it was allocated to Feltham. July 1951 saw the loco moved to Redhill shed for some ten years, moving back to Feltham in June 1961. During December 1964 it was moved to Eastleigh very briefly, being back at Feltham by January 1965, where it remained until withdrawn in September 1965. It was stored at Feltham until August 1966, though in the meantime it was reinstated to work two special trains, LCGB's 'The S15 Commemorative Rail Tour', which ran on 9 and 16 January 1966.

British Railways Standard 3MT 2-6-0 No. 77014 ended up allocated to the Southern Region and here has just arrived at Windsor & Eton Riverside station on Saturday 16 April 1966 with the RCTS 'Longmoor Rail Tour', as part of that train's itinerary on the way back from Bordon to Waterloo. This engine had taken over from LMR WD 2-10-0 No. AD600 *Gordon*, at Staines Loop. The train then returned to Waterloo behind double-headed 2-6-0s Nos. 31411 and 31639.

No. 77014 was built at BR Swindon Works in 1954 and its first

allocation was to Darlington in July of that year. It spent most of its short career at various sheds in the north-east, including Whitby, Tyne Dock and Thornaby, before being transferred from Stourton to Northwich in October 1964. From there it headed south to Guildford in March 1966 and was withdrawn from there in July 1967. It was stored at Weymouth for some time before ending up at Bird's, Risca, by December 1967 where it was scrapped by February 1968.

The RCTS 'Longmoor Rail Tour' was worked back from Windsor and Eton Riverside by 2-6-0s N Class 31411 and U Class 31639. The former engine is obscured by steam as the double-header prepares to depart from Windsor for the final leg of the tour back to Waterloo, on Saturday 16 April 1966.

The RCTS 'Longmoor Rail Tour' ran twice in April 1966 due to great demand. The second tour ran in glorious sunshine on Saturday 30 April 1966, and as part of the return itinerary the train traversed the branch to Windsor & Eton Riverside with Standard Class 5MT No. 73114 at the head (out of sight inside the train shed). The train was then hauled back to Waterloo by double-headed Class U 2-6-0s Nos. 31791 and 31639. Here they bask in the evening sunshine, overlooked by the Round Tower of Windsor Castle.

N Class 2-6-0 No. 31842, fitted with BR Standard type chimney, sits outside the small Southern Region loco shed at Reading, between duties on Saturday 22 May 1965. The SR station and shed was at a lower level than the GWR station, which can just be seen in the background above the car. Both shed and station were later demolished and SR trains were diverted via a new spur into the GWR station.

No. 31842 spent most of its BR career allocated to Exmouth Junction and Barnstaple Junction sheds, alternating between the two, until transferred to Guildford shed in mid-1964. It was withdrawn from Guildford in September 1965 and scrapped at Cashmore's, Newport in November 1965. The shed at Reading was built by the South Eastern Railway in 1852 and replaced by a newer building in 1875; it closed along with Reading Southern station in 1965.

From the Geoff Plumb Collection of original slides, photographer unknown, but possibly E.A.S. Cotton. Maunsell L1 class 4-4-0 No. 31782 was built in Glasgow during April 1926 as North British No. 23363, spending much of its career working from Bricklayers Arms depot, then transferring to Ashford during September 1953 and to Nine Elms in June 1959. It was withdrawn in February 1961 from 70A Nine Elms MPD and scrapped at Ashford Works in May 1961.

Instead of a 70A shedcode plate the engine is still carrying a 74A plate – Ashford MPD's previous code – but this had changed to 73F in October 1958. The loco is facing 'Schools' Class V 4-4-0 No. 30933 *King's Canterbury* and is ahead of D1 class 4-4-0 No. 31487. They are standing on the scrap line at Ashford Works during an RCTS visit on Sunday 19 March 1961.

From the Geoff Plumb Collection of original slides, photographer unknown, but possibly E.A.S. Cotton. SER Wainwright O1 Class 0-6-0 No. 31065 was built in 1896 at Ashford Works and had latterly been a regular performer on the KESR for many years until closure. Withdrawn from service in June 1961 from Dover shed, it eventually made it into preservation. The engine stands in the works yard at Ashford in undercoat for its elaborate SECR livery alongside BRCW 'Crompton' Class 33 diesel No. D6596, on Sunday 17 July 1966.

From the Geoff Plumb Collection of original slides, photographer unknown, but possilbly E.A.S. Cotton. The chalked legends on the engine and tender running plates say it all: 'Journeys End the Last Trip R.I.P.', as Wainwright Class C 0-6-0 No. DS 239 returns to Ashford Wagon Works Yard on Saturday 8 October 1966.

The engine had been transferred as 31592 from Stewarts Lane during 1962 and was renumbered into Departmental Stock as DS 239 in July 1963. Withdrawn in January 1966 it soldiered on until October, as seen here, prior to final withdrawal and, normally, scrap. In this case, however, the loco ended up in the preservationists' hands and was eventually returned to working order as SECR No. 592.

From the Geoff Plumb Collection of original slides, photographer unknown, but possibly E.A.S. Cotton. SR V Class 'Schools' 4-4-0 No. 30935 *Sevenoaks* is one of a line-up of locos alongside the turntable and station at Margate, perhaps having arrived on excursion trains from London, on Sunday 19 March 1961, a couple of years after electrification of the Kent lines in this area.

Built at Eastleigh in May 1935, 30935 had spent much of its BR career based at Bricklayers Arms shed, with a couple of short transfers to St. Leonards. It was transferred from Bricklayers Arms to Ashford in early 1959, then to Nine Elms later in 1961 after steam was virtually eliminated from the Kent area. It was withdrawn in December 1962 and stored at Nine Elms until March 1964. It then headed north to Cohen's at Kettering, where it was scrapped during May 1964.

From the Geoff Plumb Collection of original slides, photographer unknown, but possibly E.A.S. Cotton. Unrebuilt Bulleid 'West Country' class 4-6-2 No. 34092 *City of Wells* (originally simply *Wells*) simmers between duties at Dover, on Sunday 19 March 1961. The loco still has the old type BR crest on the original style high sided tender, whereas the diesel shunter beyond has the new style crest, introduced from 1956. The diesel is Class 04 No. D2278, which was withdrawn in April 1970 and scrapped by Pounds Ltd of Fratton at Stratford TMD in January 1971.

City of Wells became known as 'The Volcano' due to prodigious displays of exhaust when hard at work. The loco was built at Brighton

Works in 1949 and was allocated to Stewarts Lane MPD (73A) for most of its life, until transferred to Salisbury soon after this photo was taken. The red-painted parts of the motion around the slide-bars indicate the engine has had some attention in the small works at Bricklayers Arms as this was their 'trade mark'. It was withdrawn from Salisbury in November 1964 and moved to Woodham's at Barry in February 1965. It was then purchased for preservation by the Keighley & Worth Valley Railway in October 1971 and restored to working order. After many years out of use *City of Wells* is back in service, again fitted with the high sided tender.

SECR H Class 0-4-4T No. 263 (SR No. 1263 and BR No. 31263) was the last survivor of the class of sixty-six engines designed by Wainwright and built at Ashford between 1904 and 1909, the last two examples being built in 1915. Most of the engines were fitted with push-pull equipment for branch line working, all were fitted with vacuum brakes and thirteen members also had Westinghouse brakes.

No. 31263 was withdrawn from Three Bridges shed on 4 January 1964 and remained in store there until the following November, it was then purchased by the H Class Trust and moved to Robertsbridge on the fledgling Kent & East Sussex line. It is seen here on Sunday 15 May 1966 in the station yard adjacent to the BR line, where initial work is being undertaken on its preservation. It was later moved to Ashford at the South Eastern Steam Centre but moved again in 1975 to the Bluebell Railway and restored to working order.

London, Brighton and South Coast Railway A1X Class 'Terrier Tank' 0-6-0T No. 32650 sits in the sidings of the Kent & East Sussex Railway alongside Robertsbridge BR station on Sunday 15 May 1966, having recently been purchased for preservation. Built at Brighton Works in December 1876 as Class A1 No. 50 *Whitechapel*, it was rebuilt as Class A1X in May 1920.

The engine went to the Isle of Wight in May 1930 where it became No. W9 *Fishbourne*, until returning to the mainland in 1936 and stored for a while, it was then taken into Departmental Stock in 1937 as 515S at Lancing Carriage Works, where it later became DS515 *C & W Lancing Works* under BR. It returned to Capital Stock in November 1951 and

was renumbered 32650 in July/August 1953 and based at Fratton MPD.

Transferred to Eastleigh in November 1959, it was one of the regular locos working the branch to Hayling Island, all of which were withdrawn when the line closed in November 1963, by which time they were the oldest locos working on BR. Stored at Eastleigh until May 1964, the engine was bought by the Borough of Sutton & Cheam (now the London Borough of Sutton & Merton). It went to the KESR to be restored on condition that it carried the number 10 and name *Sutton*. After restoration the loco was one of the two involved in the haulage of reopening day public services on the line in June 1974. The loco is now on the Spa Valley Railway as No. 50 *Sutton*.

After withdrawal in April 1961, ex-SECR P Class 0-6-0T No. 31556 was sold to James Hodson (Millers) & Sons Ltd in June 1961 for use at a flour mill in Robertsbridge, where it was repainted and named *Pride of Sussex* to shunt the sidings connected to the KESR and BR. The loco was still in occasional use until rail traffic to the mill ceased from January 1970 and the engine was sold to the KESR, becoming No. 11 for a while. It is shown here on Sunday 15 May 1966.

The engine was the first of eight, designed by H.S. Wainwright and built at Ashford Works as SECR No. 753, entering service on 18 February 1909 and based at Tonbridge shed. From April 1915 to October 1916, No. 753 worked in Boulogne as part of the war effort as ROD No. 5753.

After collision damage the engine returned to England and by 1923 was carriage pilot at Redhill, being renumbered 556 at the end of 1925 and A556 from November 1926. Its final SR number was 1556, applied around July 1931. 1556 was hired to the KESR during 1936 and again in 1938, to cover loco shortages on the line.

It then returned to the Dover and Folkestone area for work around the harbours, where it had been based during the late 1920s, and also spent some time based at Gillingham. It was hired to the KESR again during 1947 and under BR became No. 31556. By 1953 the engine was based at Brighton working as shed pilot and also at Shoreham Harbour.

Unrebuilt Bulleid SR 'Battle of Britain' Class 4-6-2 No. 34066 *Spitfire* sits in the platform on Sunday 22 March 1964 at Tunbridge Wells West station with the joint RCTS/LCGB 'The Sussex Downsman' Railtour. This engine took over the train here from Q1 0-6-0 No. 33027 and worked it through Eridge and Hailsham along the 'Cuckoo Line', just a year prior to closure, to Pevensey and Westham. Part of this line was later reopened by the Tunbridge Wells & Eridge Railway Preservation Society and is now the Spa Valley Railway, based at Tunbridge Wells West.

The engine was built at Brighton Works and emerged as 21C166 in

September 1947 and spent its first couple of years based at Ramsgate shed. Renumbered 34066 (February 1949) after nationalisation it moved on to Stewarts Lane depot from December 1949 and remained there until transfer to Exmouth Junction in January 1961. Salisbury was its final allocation from September 1964 and it was withdrawn two years later, having covered 652,908 miles in service. Stored at Basingstoke Yard and Salisbury until December 1966, it arrived at Buttigieg's, Newport, in January 1967 and was scrapped by September 1967.

Introduced from 1913, Billinton LBSCR Class K 2-6-0 No. 32341 is a Brighton (75A) allocated engine and is here standing round the back of Three Bridges MPD on Sunday 1 April 1962. I saw all but two of the seventeen strong class, but this was the only one I managed to photograph. The engine was built at Brighton Works in November 1914 and spent most of its career based at Brighton; it was withdrawn from there in December 1962 and stored for a while at Hove Goods Yard. Moved to Eastleigh around June 1963, it was scrapped there during August 1963. Sadly, none of the class survived into preservation.

Bulleid Q1 class 0-6-0 No. 33027 is at the head of the joint RCTS/LCGB 'The Sussex Downsman' Railtour. Having started from Waterloo station on Sunday 22 March 1964, it is now standing at Cranleigh en route to Horsham where a loco change took place and the tour reversed direction of travel.

Cranleigh was on the LBSCR Horsham & Guildford line from Peasmarsh Junction, south of Guildford on the Portsmouth Direct Line, through Bramley & Wonersh, Baynards, Rudgwick and Slinfold to Stammerham Junction, near Christ's Hospital, where it joined the Shoreham & Horsham line and the Mid-Sussex line. The station was opened on 2 October 1865, originally as Cranley, and renamed Cranleigh in 1867, apparently at the request of the Postmaster General, to avoid confusion with Crawley! The line and its stations closed from 14 June 1965 under Beeching's *The Reshaping of British Railways* report of 1963.

South Eastern and Chatham Railway Class N 2-6-0 31411 took over the joint RCTS/LCGB 'The Sussex Downsman' Railtour train at Horsham, reversing direction to Itchingfield Junction and then along the now abandoned line through West Grinstead and Steyning to Shoreham. The train is stopped here at Partridge Green station, possibly for water and a photo opportunity, on Sunday 22 March 1964.

Class N was designed by R.E.L. Maunsell for the SECR and built from 1917 to 1923. The original fifteen at Ashford Works were followed by another fifty engines assembled from parts made by Woolwich Arsenal,

the boilers from North British and assembled at Ashford in 1923–24. A further batch of fifteen locos, including No. 1411, was built with modified 4,000 gallon tenders at Ashford in 1932–34. At this stage of its career, 31411 was a Redhill allocated engine, moving to Guildford in January 1965 and withdrawn from there in April 1966. Stored at Guildford until August 1966 it was scrapped at Cashmore's, Newport in September 1966. Partridge Green station closed along with the Steyning line from 7 March 1966, another casualty of the 'Beeching Axe'.

Unrebuilt Bulleid SR 'Battle of Britain' Class 4-6-2 No. 34066 *Spitfire* sits in the platform at Hailsham station on Sunday 22 March 1964 with the joint RCTS/LCGB 'The Sussex Downsman' Railtour. This engine took over the train at Tunbridge Wells West and worked it through Eridge and Hailsham along the 'Cuckoo Line', just over a year prior to closure, to Pevensey & Westham. Tour participants pile off the train to take photos – some of them not bothering with the platforms!

Hailsham was opened on 14 May 1849, originally as a terminus on the LBSCR line from Polegate Junction. It became a through station from September 1880 when the line was extended northwards to Eridge through Hellingly and Heathfield. When the line north of Hailsham closed to passengers from 14 March 1965, it became a terminus once again, though goods traffic continued to Heathfield until 26 April 1968. Traffic stopped just short of the closure due date of 7 May, after a lorry hit a bridge near Horsebridge, north of Hailsham, and it was not deemed economical to repair it. Passenger services from Hailsham ceased completely from 9 September 1968 and the line from Polegate Junction closed. Much of the trackbed between Polegate and Heathfield today forms the 'Cuckoo Trail' cycle and footpath.

The RCTS/LCGB 'The Sussex Downsman' Railtour has arrived at Pevensey & Westham station via the 'Cuckoo Line' through Hailsham on Sunday 22 March 1964 behind unrebuilt 'West Country' Class 4-6-2 No. 34066 *Spitfire* from Tunbridge Wells West. The train is now reversing direction and N class 2-6-0 No. 31411 is taking over once again for the run to Lewes and Brighton. Pevensey & Westham on the LBSCR Hastings to Lewes line opened in 1851 and is now part of the East Coastway Line, operated by Southern (Govia Thameslink Railway).

South Eastern and Chatham Railway Maunsell N Class 2-6-0 No. 31411 is in charge of the joint RCTS/LCGB 'The Sussex Downsman' Railtour on Sunday 22 March 1964. Here it is visiting the site of the original terminal station at Lewes Friars Walk, by this time Lewes East Sidings, before making its way to Brighton. No. 31411 had taken over the train again at Pevensey & Westham station, where it had reversed after arriving from Tunbridge Wells West behind unrebuilt 'Battle of Britain' 4-6-2 No. 34066 *Spitfire*.

N Class 2-6-0 No. 31411 is at the head of the joint RCTS/LCGB 'The Sussex Downsman' Railtour on Sunday 22 March 1964, at the site of Lewes Friars Walk station, by this time known as Lewes East Sidings. The original station in Lewes was built as a terminus in 1846 at Friars Walk for the line from Brighton. Separate through platforms were provided nearby at Pinwell for through trains to Hastings and a halt was built at Southover (also known as Ham).

This arrangement was very unsatisfactory and a new station was built in November 1857 with through platforms at the junction of the Brighton lines and the lines to Keymer Junction, Friars Walk then becoming a goods terminal. The new station itself was replaced by yet another arrangement, on the same site, from 1889 when the Hastings and Uckfield lines were re-aligned. The Uckfield line was closed from 4 May 1969 and associated earthworks and bridges were quickly demolished as part of the Lewes Relief Road scheme. The Friars Walk goods yard was abandoned at the same time.

From the Geoff Plumb Collection of original slides, photographer unknown. LSWR Adams T3 Class 4-4-0 No. 563, preserved in Drummond's 1903 livery, sits in lovely sunshine at Brighton shed on the afternoon of 13 April 1958. This was one of twenty engines constructed at Nine Elms Works in 1892/93; very successful and fast runners with their 6ft 7in driving wheels, they were to be found all over the LSWR lines. All twenty were taken into Southern Railway stock in 1923, though all but three had been withdrawn by 1933.

No. 557 was withdrawn in 1936, 571 succumbed in 1943, followed by 563 in August 1945 with over 1½ mllion miles under its belt. It survived long enough to represent the old LSWR at an exhibition to celebrate the centenary of Waterloo station in 1948. Afterwards it was stored at Farnham electric carriage shed and moved during 1958 for further storage at Tweedmouth – perhaps the photo was taken during this move? Once Clapham Museum was opened it was put on display there and subsequently at York Museum; it is now at Shildon after returning from Toronto, Ontario, where it appeared in a production of 'The Railway Children' at the Roundhouse Park during 2011.

On Sunday 22 March 1964, the RCTS and LCGB ran a joint special, 'The Sussex Downsman' Railtour, from London Waterloo via diverse routes to Brighton and return via Uckfield to London Victoria. Unrebuilt Bulleid 'Battle of Britain' Class 4-6-2 No. 34066 *Spitfire* awaits departure time at Brighton, admired by some of the tour participants.

This loco was involved in the accident at St. John's, Lewisham on 4 December 1957, when the train it was hauling ran into the back of an electric train in dense fog. Sadly, 90 persons lost their lives and over a hundred were injured. The loco was repaired and back in service by 22 March 1958. Brighton station was opened by the London & Brighton Railway in May 1840 for trains to Shoreham and September 1841 for trains to London. In 1846, after various mergers, the station became part of the LBSCR.

London, Midland and Scottish Railway Ivatt 2MT 2-6-2T No. 41287 worked the joint RCTS/LCGB 'The Sussex Downsman' Railtour on Sunday 22 March 1964 from Brighton to the terminus of the short branch to Kemp Town, where it is seen after running round the train prior to returning to Brighton station.

The line to Kemp Town was built by the LBSCR, mainly to prevent the rival LCDR from doing so! It was opened on 2 August 1869, branching off the line to Lewes only a short distance from the main station in Brighton. Just over a mile in length, the line took five years to build and was very expensive as much of it is either on viaducts and embankments or in a tunnel.

Lewes Road station was very close to the junction with the main line. At the terminus there was an extensive layout but the station itself had only one platform. Services were suspended during the First World War, passenger trains returning from August 1919 and goods three years later. Never a success, the line lost its passenger trains completely from 1 January 1933, although goods traffic continued until June 1971.

The joint RCTS/LCGB 'The Sussex Downsman' Railtour visited the terminus of the branch line to Kemp Town in Brighton on Sunday 22 March 1964 as part of its itinerary. Here, LMS Ivatt 2MT 2-6-2T No. 41287 faces the 1,024 yard Kemp Town tunnel through Race Hill, leading back to the main line before returning to Brighton. After closure, the tunnel was used for a while as a mushroom farm; this portal is now in part of an industrial estate and used to store vehicles, while the northern portal is blocked up.

No. 41287, though an LMS design, was built at Crewe Works by BR in November 1950, one of the class fitted with push-pull equipment. It started life allocated to Crewe North before spending the next few years at Sutton Oak, Rhyl and Bangor, then moving to Patricroft in October 1954. It was transferred to the Southern Region and moved to Brighton in June 1961, transferring again to Guildford just a month or so after this photo was taken. Eastleigh became its final home from June 1965 and it was withdrawn in July 1966. Stored at Eastleigh until October 1966, it was sold to Cohen's, Morriston, Swansea, where it was scrapped during November 1966.

My very first photograph, taken on my father's Box Brownie camera! Ex-LBSCR Marsh H2 Class 4-4-2 'Brighton Atlantic' No. 32424 *Beachy Head* at Newhaven with the RCTS 'Sussex Coast' Railtour on Sunday 13 April 1958. The engine was built at Brighton Works in September 1911, entering service as No. 2424. Having become the last 'Atlantic' running in normal service in the country, this was the engine's final trip in passenger service. After this tour the engine worked light to Brighton and then hauled a twelve coach train of carriages from Lancing to Eastleigh Carriage Works and was then withdrawn from service.

No. 32424 was allocated to Newhaven and Brighton for all of its BR career, alternating between the two, its final allocation being to Brighton from June 1955. Reluctant to cut up the engine in case moves were moved to preserve it, the scrapmen at Eastleigh delayed their efforts as long as possible, the loco finally succumbing on 26 May 1958. Ironically, a new-build version of the loco is now being constructed at the Bluebell Railway.

Southern Railway unrebuilt Bulleid 'Battle of Britain' Class 4-6-2 No. 34083 *605 Squadron* restarts its Plymouth to Brighton train away from the station stop at Cosham, on Tuesday 18 February 1964. The engine was built at Brighton Works under BR, entering service in November 1948 at Stewarts Lane, then moving to Ramsgate shed in June 1951. Dover was its next allocation, from January 1958 then moving on to Ashford for a short time from May 1961. Its last re-allocation was to Exmouth Junction during October 1961, remaining there until withdrawal in July 1964. Stored until October it moved on to Severn Tunnel Junction during November 1964 and finally to R.S. Hayes/Bird's, Tremains Yard, Bridgend in January 1965, though not meeting its end until October 1965.

From the Geoff Plumb Collection of original slides, photo by D.E. White. Ex-LBSCR 'Terrier' Class A1X 0-6-0T No. 32678 pauses at North Hayling station with a train from Havant to Hayling Island on the afternoon of Thursday 4 May 1961. No. 32678 was originally a Class A1 introduced by Stroudley in 1872–1880, this engine being built at Brighton Works in July 1880. The class was modified to A1X from 1911.

This engine was originally No. 78 *Knowle* then carried the name *Bembridge* whilst working on the Isle of Wight, firstly as W4 from July 1929 and as W14 from 1932. Returned to the mainland in May 1936 and withdrawn in December 1936, it was reprieved and reboilered,

becoming SR No. 2678 and hired to the KESR during 1940, also working there in early BR days as No. 32678. It was finally withdrawn from service in October 1963 from Brighton and stored until May 1964 at Eastleigh. It was one of eight 'Terriers' that made it into preservation, initially at Butlin's Holiday Camp in Minehead on static display and sold on to the adjacent West Somerset Railway in 1975. Sold again to Resco (Railways) in April 1983 it returned to the KESR and is still in working order some 136 years after being built! The Hayling Island branch was closed in 1963, being worked by A1X tanks right up until the end. The trackbed is now the 'Hayling Billy' trail footpath and cycleway.

From the Geoff Plumb Collection of original slides, photo by T.J. Edgington. SR U Class 2-6-0 No. 31639 at Gosport with the RCTS 'The Solent Rail Tour' on Sunday 20 March 1966. This engine worked the tour from Fareham to Gosport, where it has just run round the train before returning to Fareham. There it was joined by BR Standard 4MT 4-6-0 No. 75070 to work double-headed by a circuitous route back to Waterloo.

Gosport was a rather grand terminus station designed by William

Tite and opened by the LSWR in 1841. Initially very busy with both passengers and freight, it declined after the First World War and despite a revival during the Second World War it eventually closed to passengers on 6 June 1953, although goods traffic continued until 30 January 1969. The main station building has a Grade II* listing and has been incorporated into a housing development for the Guinness Trust.

Southern Railway U Class 2-6-0s Nos. 31791 & 31639 have just arrived at Woking station on Saturday 30 April 1966 with an RCTS special, 'The Longmoor Rail Tour' from Waterloo and are now coming off the train to be replaced by Longmoor Military Railway WD 2-10-0 No. AD600 *Gordon* for the run to Liss and onto the Longmoor system. The Health & Safety regime was somewhat more relaxed in those days; even so a railway official keeps a watchful eye on the photographers!

An unusual sight on BR tracks was Longmoor Military Railway WD 2-10-0 No. AD600 *Gordon*, here seen at Woking on Saturday 30 April 1966 whilst waiting to take over the RCTS 'The Longmoor Rail Tour' which had arrived from Waterloo behind two SR U Class 2-6-0s. *Gordon* headed the tour from Woking onto the LMR at Liss.

Gordon was built by North British at the Hyde Park Works in Glasgow in 1943, Works No. 25437, and was named after General Charles Gordon ('Gordon of Khartoum') of the Royal Engineers. After the Longmoor Military Railway finally closed in 1969, and after a preservation attempt failed, the engine was moved to the Severn Valley Railway during 1972, where it became operational for some years before moving into the 'Engine House' at Highley.

The RCTS 'Longmoor Rail Tour' train had been hauled by 'Austerity' 0-6-0ST No. AD196 into the LMR station at Bordon on Saturday 30 April 1966 with WD 2-10-0 No. AD600 *Gordon* on the rear of the train before reversal. AD196 can be seen in the background in the LMR station and *Gordon* has shunted the stock from the LMR into the former SR station, before departing for Bentley and Staines.

The branch line from Bentley to Bordon was built under the Light Railways Act of 1896 by the LSWR with the help of the War Department, opening in 1905, mainly in order to carry troops and materials to Bordon Camp. There was a sparse passenger and goods service as well as the military traffic. When the Woolmer Instructional Railway (later the Longmoor Military Railway) was extended to Bordon in the same year, there were two stations alongside each other for exchange traffic. Passenger services ceased from 16 September 1957 and the line closed completely from 4 April 1966, just prior to these specials running on 16 and 30 April 1966, the track being lifted later the same year.

The driver of rebuilt 'West Country' Class 4-6-2 No. 34012 *Launceston* looks back, waiting for the guard's green flag before departing from Fleet station with the 11:54 stopping train from Waterloo to Basingstoke on Saturday 24 April 1965. Note the wonderful lower quadrant LSWR signals on the gantry that were pneumatically operated.

The loco was built at Brighton Works, going into service as 21C112 from October 1945. It was named on 1 November 1945 at Launceston by the Mayor, Alderman G.E. Trood JP, and renumbered to 34012 after nationalisation in 1948 at which time it was an Exmouth Junction

engine, soon moving to Plymouth Friary until 1950. It moved back to Exmouth Junction and then Salisbury for a while before a spell at Nine Elms until October 1957 when it was rebuilt at Eastleigh Works by January 1958.

Bricklayers Arms became its next home before moving again to Brighton in June 1962 and back to Salisbury during June 1963, its home depot at the time of this picture. Its final reallocation was to Bournemouth from October 1965 from where it was withdrawn during December 1966. Stored at Eastleigh until March 1967, it was finally taken to Cashmore's Newport, where it was scrapped by June 1967.

It wasn't all glamour jobs for the Bulleid Pacifics! Unrebuilt 'West Country' Class 4-6-2 No. 34006 *Bude* still carries its nameplates but is in filthy condition, as it approaches Fleet station on Saturday 24 April 1965 with a down ballast train, perhaps returning to Meldon Quarry for reloading.

The loco was built at Brighton Works and emerged as 21C106 in August 1945, being named at Bude on 1 November 1945 by Councillor J.H. Hallett, Chairman, Bude & Stratton Urban District Council. After nationalisation it became 34006 in May 1948 and based at Exmouth Junction shed until March 1951.

No. 34006 was one of three 'WC' Class Pacifics used in the 1948 Locomotive Exchange Trials organised by the newly formed British Railways, ostensibly to compare engines from the 'Big Four' to establish best practice for the forthcoming BR Standard designs, but in actuality rather more of a publicity stunt. *Bude* worked over the former GWR route from Bristol to Plymouth via Taunton and also on the former Great Central route from Marylebone to Manchester. The locos were attached to LMS tenders (as were the 'Merchant Navies' involved in the trials) so that they could pick up water on the move – SR tenders having no scoops as there were no water troughs on the Southern. For some reason, they also acquired considerably longer smoke deflectors as part of the 'air-smoothed casing', which *Bude* is still carrying in the photo.

After the trials the loco returned to Exmouth Junction, moving on to Nine Elms in March 1951 where it remained until a final move to Salisbury in September 1964. Withdrawn in March 1967 it was stored at Salisbury until August, finally going to Cashmore's Newport, and being scrapped in September 1967.

Rebuilt Bulleid 'Merchant Navy' 4-6-2 No. 35008 *Orient Line* races south passing Fleet with a down express from Waterloo to Bournemouth on Saturday 24 April 1965. Built at Eastleigh Works, the loco entered service in June 1942 as No. 21C8 and was named on 2 November 1942, and at nationalisation it was based at Salisbury.

It was renumbered to 35008 in July 1949 and transferred to Bournemouth for a short while from around February 1954, before moving on again to Exmouth Junction in the period ending on 20 August 1954. It returned to Eastleigh for rebuilding during May 1957 and it was back as a Bournemouth engine again by March 1960, remaining there until October 1966, and then becoming a Weymouth engine. Its final transfer was to Nine Elms in April 1967 and it survived until the end of steam in July 1967. It moved for storage back to Salisbury until March 1968 and ended up for scrap at Buttigieg's, Newport, meeting its end by October 1968.

Rebuilt Bulleid 'Merchant Navy' Class 4-6-2 No. 35023 *Holland–Afrika Line* near Fleet with a down Bournemouth express on Saturday 24 April 1965. It is passing some disused platforms – the remains of Bramshot Halt, by this time long closed. This was a request stop used by golfers of the nearby Bramshot Golf Club, opened in 1905, the Halt opening on 1 May 1913. Only members of the Golf Club could use the halt until 3 July 1938.

The course was requisitioned by the Air Ministry in 1940 and never re-opened after the war, the clubhouse buildings being demolished in the 1980s. The railway halt closed after the Second World War in 1946 after some workers constructing the nearby Southwood Army Camp were killed whilst trying to cross the tracks. Here, conductor rails for the electrification of the line are in place on the slow lines, but not yet on the fast lines.

Rebuilt 'Merchant Navy' Class 4-6-2 No. 35013 *Blue Funnel* is in charge of a Bournemouth line train as it speeds through Fleet station on the down fast line on the afternoon of Saturday 24 April 1965. Built as 21C13 at Eastleigh Works in February 1945, it had been named on 17 April 1945, and was allocated to Nine Elms at nationalisation in January 1948.

Renumbered to 35013 in August 1948, it was transferred to Exmouth Junction during March 1954 and was rebuilt at Eastleigh Works in May 1956, returning to Exmouth Junction until September 1964. Bournemouth was its next home depot followed by Weymouth from October 1966. Its final transfer was to Nine Elms in February 1967 and it was withdrawn from there in July 1967. Stored at Salisbury until February 1968 it was scrapped at Buttigieg's, Newport, during March 1968.

Rebuilt 'Battle of Britain' Class 4-6-2 No. 34082 *615 Squadron* waits departure time at Fleet station on Saturday 24 April 1965 with the 17:40 Basingstoke to Waterloo stopping train under clear signals – note the repeater arm low down on the gantry.

No. 34082 was built by BR at Brighton Works, entering service in September 1948, spending the first nine years of its life allocated to Ramsgate MPD. Moved to Stewarts Lane in January 1958, it was soon back in Kent, transferred to Dover in March 1958 and then to Nine Elms from May 1961, in the meantime having been rebuilt at Eastleigh Works in April 1960. Its final re-allocation was to Eastleigh during September 1964 and it was withdrawn in April 1966. Stored at Eastleigh until September 1966, it was scrapped the following month at Cashmore's, Newport.

British Railways (Southern Region) rebuilt Bulleid 'Battle of Britain' Class 4-6-2 No. 34109 *Sir Trafford Leigh-Mallory* rushes through Winchfield station on the down fast line with an express from Waterloo to Bournemouth on Saturday 4 July 1964.

Built by BR at Brighton Works in May 1950, 34109 entered service as a Bournemouth allocated loco. Transferred to Exmouth Junction from February 1958 it was rebuilt at Eastleigh Works in March 1961, returning to Exmouth Junction until its withdrawal a mere three years later in September 1964. It was stored at Exmouth Junction until November 1964 and scrapped by Bird's, Morriston, Swansea in January 1965, after a service life of just 14 years and 4 months.

Winchfield station was originally a temporary terminus when opened as Shapley Heath by the London & Southampton Railway on 24 September 1838 as it extended its line from Woking. By June the following year the line was opened to Basingstoke, the terminus becoming a through station and renamed Winchfield by November 1840. The island platform for the fast lines was long disused, though it did house the signal box at the time of the photo. Both this and the platform are now long gone.

British Railways Standard 4MT 4-6-0 No. 75076 heads south west through Winchfield Cutting on Saturday 11 April 1964 with a long train of four-wheel vans, its headcode discs suggesting a working from Nine Elms to Southampton Docks via Brentford, Chertsey and Woking. The engine is one of the class fitted with a double-chimney.

No. 75076 was built at Swindon Works in December 1955 and was initially allocated to Exmouth Junction shed. A Southern Region engine for all of its short life, it was a Nine Elms shedded loco at this time. Transferred to Eastleigh in mid-1965 it was withdrawn from there in July 1967 and after a short period in store at Weymouth it was scrapped at Bird's, Risca in December 1967.

Rebuilt 'Battle of Britain' Class 4-6-2 No. 34059 *Sir Archibald Sinclair* accelerates away from the call on Saturday 11 April 1964 at Winchfield station on the down slow line through Winchfield cutting with a Basingstoke local stopper consisting of four coaches and a couple of vans. The train is passing the point at which the M3 roadbridge now crosses the cutting. At this stage there is no sign of the forthcoming electrification and the down slow line is still laid with bullhead rails.

No. 34059 was built at Brighton Works in April 1947 as 21C159 and spent its early BR career at Nine Elms depot before moving to Exmouth Junction in early 1951, moving again to Salisbury in late 1955. Rebuilt during March 1960 it remained at Salisbury until withdrawal in May 1966 and was then stored for a few months at Eastleigh. Sold to Woodham's at Barry, the loco spent some thirteen years there before being sold for preservation in October 1979 and is now on the Bluebell Railway.

Filthy dirty BR Standard 5MT 4-6-0 No. 73111 *King Uther* is working an up Basingstoke to Waterloo 'stopper' on Saturday 11 April 1964, comprising Bulleid coaching stock, and has shut off to drift towards Winchfield station as it passes under Potbridge Road bridge in Winchfield Cutting. This class was designed at Doncaster Works but the majority of the 172 engines were constructed at Derby Works between 1951 and 1957.

No. 73111 was one of 42 built at Doncaster and was outshopped in October 1955. It was allocated to Nine Elms depot for most of its very short life, being transferred to Eastleigh in the latter part of 1964 and it was withdrawn from there in September 1965. Stored until January 1966 at Eastleigh it was then taken to Cashmore's, Newport, where it was scrapped during February 1966. Twenty of the Southern Region locos were named during 1959, taking the names of some of the 'King Arthur' N15 Class 4-6-0s then being withdrawn.

Rebuilt Bulleid 'Battle of Britain' Class 4-6-2 No. 34053 *Sir Keith Park* heads south west through Winchfield Cutting on Saturday 11 April 1964 with a long train of vans on the down slow line at about the point where the M3 motorway bridge now crosses the line. The headcode would suggest a working from Nine Elms to Southampton Docks via Brentford, Chertsey and Woking.

Built at Brighton Works as 21C153 in January 1947 it was renumbered 34053 on 25 June 1949, whilst allocated to Salisbury depot. At nationalisation it was a Salisbury engine, moving to Stewarts Lane for a short while from March 1948 until December 1948 when it

moved back to Salisbury. Further brief periods in the early 1950s saw it allocated to Nine Elms and Exmouth Junction, returning to Salisbury by June 1951. It remained there until transferred to Bournemouth in November 1958, after being rebuilt at Eastleigh Works, and it saw out its days there until withdrawal in October 1965. Stored at Bournemouth and then Eastleigh until December 1965, by February 1966 it was at Woodham's, Barry, from where it was eventually sold to Charles Timms in 1979, rescued in June 1984 and finally preserved by Southern Locomotives Ltd and now back in working order.

Rebuilt 'West Country' Class 4-6-2 No. 34095 *Brentor* heads south west through Winchfield Cutting on the down slow line with a stopping train to Salisbury on Saturday 4 July 1964. No. 34095 was built at Eastleigh Works and entered service on 29 October 1949, allocated originally to Ramsgate, though moving to Bournemouth by the middle of December 1949. It became a Nine Elms engine from January 1956 and returned there after rebuilding at Eastleigh Works in January 1961. It was reallocated to Eastleigh from September 1964 where it remained until withdrawn at the end of steam in July 1967. Stored for a while at Weymouth until January 1968, it was scrapped by Cashmore's, Newport, during April 1968.

British Railways Standard Class 4MT 2-6-0 No. 76030 trundles along the down slow line through Winchfield Cutting on Saturday 4 July 1964 with a train of empty bogie bolster wagons, possibly bound for Basingstoke Yard. No. 76030 was built at Doncaster Works and was put into service from November 1953 at Stratford MPD, then on to Cambridge and March during 1960. It was transferred to the Southern Region from December 1962, taking up residence at Brighton shed before moving on in September 1963 to Guildford. January 1965 saw the engine moved to Eastleigh depot and it was withdrawn from there in April 1965 and was scrapped by Cashmore's, Newport, during December 1965.

Southern Railway S15 class 4-6-0 No. 30824 heads south west out of Winchfield Cutting at Potbridge Totters Lane on Saturday 11 April 1964 with a long goods train on the down slow line. According to its disc headcode, this is a working from Nine Elms to Southampton Terminus (though not a Boat Train!), but whether it went beyond Basingstoke or Eastleigh, I don't know.

No. 30824 was built at Eastleigh Works, entering service during March 1927, spending a considerable part of its life at Exmouth Junction and Salisbury sheds. By this time, it was allocated to Feltham, to where it moved in 1963 and moved on again to Eastleigh during 1965, from where it was withdrawn in September 1965. After a period in store at Feltham, it was scrapped by Cashmore's, Newport, during December 1965.

On Saturday 6 November 1965, there seemed to be an engineering possession on the fast lines through Winchfield Cutting, with all trains appearing on the slow lines. This was the first movement over the down fast line – just a light engine! This is unrebuilt 'Battle of Britain' Class 4-6-2 No. 34064 *Fighter Command* (fitted with a Giesl Ejector chimney), looking very clean and carrying a west of England line headcode.

The engine was built at Brighton Works, the 1,000th loco to be built there, emerging as 21C164 in July 1947. It was also the first SR Pacific to be built with a 'vee' shaped cab, and went to Ramsgate depot and then Stewarts Lane. From 1950 it was allocated to Nine Elms depot and

it carried experimental apple green livery from June 1948 to June 1950 as part of the BR livery trials.

Some three years were spent allocated to Exmouth Junction until mid-1962 when it returned to Nine Elms. The Giesl Ejector was fitted in April 1962 and did enhance the engine's performance considerably, but as with so many such improvements it came too late to make a real difference for the class. The loco was reallocated to Eastleigh in late 1963 and moved on to Salisbury from 25 October 1965, just a couple of weeks before this picture was taken. It was withdrawn in May 1966 and stored at Basingstoke Yard for a few months before being scrapped at Bird's, Bridgend, during November 1966.

Southern Railway rebuilt 'West Country' Class 4-6-2 No. 34048 *Crediton* (though its nameplates have been removed) is working a down Basingstoke semi-fast along the slow line at Potbridge, between Winchfield and Hook on the lovely sunny day of Saturday 6 November 1965.

The engine was built at Brighton Works and it entered service from November 1946, numbered 21C148. At nationalisation in 1948 it was a Salisbury engine, moving to Exmouth Junction later that year. By 1951 it was back at Salisbury, then moving to Brighton later in 1951. After rebuilding at Eastleigh Works in March 1959 it became a Bournemouth engine for a short period, finally reallocated to Salisbury for the remainder of its existence from mid-1960 until withdrawal in March 1966. Stored at Eastleigh until July 1966, it then moved on for further storage at Dock Street Goods Yard in Newport before finally succumbing at Cashmore's, Newport, in September 1966.

British Railways (Southern Region) 'Merchant Navy' Class 4-6-2 No. 35022 *Holland–America Line* is at the head of an up express from Bournemouth, approaching Hook on the LSWR main line on Saturday 13 March 1965. At this stage, the only sign of the impending electrification is the conductor rail on the down slow line.

No. 35022 was built at Eastleigh Works and entered service in October 1948 and its home shed was originally Exmouth Junction. It was moved to the Rugby Testing Plant during Period 3/1952 (20 March to 17 June 1952) and was based there for almost two years before moving back to Exmouth Junction around January 1954, then moving to Bournemouth a few months later. It was rebuilt at Eastleigh during

June 1956 and returned to Bournemouth for a while before going back to Exmouth Junction in early 1960 for four years or so.

Transferred to Nine Elms in February 1964 its final reallocation was to Weymouth during September of the same year. It was withdrawn from Weymouth in May 1966 and was stored there until August and then moved to Woodham's, Barry, where it remained for the next twenty years – longer than its service life! It was sold for preservation in 1983, to the Southern Steam Trust, Swanage, and left Barry during March 1986. The engine was subsequently sold to a private individual who later donated it to the Royal Scot Locomotive and General Trust, an organisation established in 2009.

On Saturday 22 May 1965 a nicely cleaned-up unrebuilt 'Battle of Britain' Class 4-6-2, No. 34051 *Winston Churchill*, has arrived at Basingstoke station with a down mixed goods train which it has worked from Nine Elms. It has caused quite a stir amongst the local enthusiasts as a clean engine was fairly rare by this time! The engine came off the train here and was replaced by a Standard Class 4 4-6-0, while 34051 went on shed. It later worked light engine to Birmingham to work a railtour (the Stephenson Locomotive Society 'Bulleid Pacific Rail Tour') the following day, presumably the reason it was so clean! It worked this train at 08:45 from Birmingham Snow Hill via Oxford, Reading and Basingstoke to Salisbury, where 35017 *Belgian Marine*

took over the train for the onward run to Westbury via Exeter and Taunton.

No. 34051 was built at Brighton Works in December 1946, entering service as SR 21C151, based at Salisbury depot. After short allocations to Nine Elms and Exmouth Junction sheds, it was back at Salisbury by June 1951, remaining there for the rest of its career. It was withdrawn in September 1965 and due to its working the funeral train of its namesake, it became part of the National Collection. It is now on display at the National Railway Museum in York, but has never steamed in preservation.

On the left, unrebuilt 'Battle of Britain' Class 4-6-2 No. 34051 *Winston Churchill* is in charge of a mixed goods train it has hauled from Nine Elms and is about to enter the yard at Basingstoke on Saturday 22 May 1965, where a Standard Class 4MT 4-6-0 will take over the train. No. 34051 would then go to the loco shed on the right of the picture before leaving again as a light engine to Birmingham for a special train the following day. On the right, 'Merchant Navy' Class 4-6-2 No. 35029 *Ellerman Lines* is arriving with the northbound 'Pines Express', Bournemouth to Manchester, which it worked as far as Reading or Oxford.

Rebuilt 'Battle of Britain' Class 4-6-2 No. 34089 *602 Squadron* nears Basingstoke on Saturday 22 May 1965 with a light-weight stopper, the 11.54 from Waterloo to Basingstoke. Built at Brighton Works in December 1948, the engine was initially allocated to Ramsgate before moving to Stewarts Lane during May 1951. Apart from the months from February to June 1952, during which it was transferred to Stratford MPD (Eastern Region, code 30A – one of several Bulleid 'Pacifics' to cover for new 'Britannia' 4-6-2s taken out of service for modifications), it remained a Stewarts Lane engine until November 1962, when it was transferred to Brighton. In the meantime, it had been rebuilt at Eastleigh in November 1960.

Its final re-allocation was to Salisbury depot in September 1963 where it remained until withdrawn in July 1967 at the end of steam on the Southern. It had been the final steam loco to be repaired at Eastleigh Works, emerging on 6 October 1966. Stored at Salisbury until March 1968, by April it was at Cashmore's, Newport, where it was scrapped during September 1968.

This caused some bewilderment when it first appeared in the distance! BR Standard 4MT 4-6-0 No. 75076 is propelling a snowplough, recently ex-works, along the down slow line as it approaches Basingstoke on Saturday 22 May 1965. Quite where it had come from or was going to I have no idea! The plough seems to be mounted on an old steam engine tender – the Southern Region did convert some old 'Schools' Class tenders into snowploughs, but this does not look like one of these.

Rebuilt 'Battle of Britain' Class 'Pacific' No. 34059 *Sir Archibald Sinclair* passes the old abandoned signal box east of Basingstoke at Barton Mill with a down Bournemouth line express on Saturday 22 May 1965. This was an LSWR Type 4 box; it opened on 25 September 1904 to replace an earlier box and was fitted with a 32-lever low-pressure pneumatic frame (pull out slides). The box closed on 22 November 1930 when Basingstoke East then worked to Hook. The signals on the down are worked by Basingstoke East (later renamed Basingstoke 'A'), the Down Fast being No. 58, the Down Slow No. 60, the distant signals being worked by Basingstoke West (later Basingstoke 'B'). Signal box details supplied by Mark Jamieson.

Rebuilt Bulleid 'Merchant Navy' 4-6-2 No. 35027 *Port Line* rumbles into Basingstoke station with a down Bournemouth express, passing a wonderful array of semaphore signals for up trains on Saturday 22 May 1965. Built at Eastleigh Works, 35027 entered service in December 1948 allocated to Bournemouth MPD, moving on to Stewarts Lane in April 1950. Transferred back to Bournemouth in June 1955 it was rebuilt at Eastleigh during May 1957, returning afterwards to Bournemouth until its withdrawal from service in September 1966. The loco worked the Royal Train from Windsor to Hamworthy Junction in April 1959.

Stored at Nine Elms and then Eastleigh until February 1967, it was bought for scrap by Woodham's and moved to Barry by March 1967. Along with many others it languished there for years, finally being sold for preservation during December 1982. After restoration took place, mainly at Blunsdon and Swindon Works by the predecessors of Southern Locomotives Ltd, the engine was based at the Bluebell Railway from 1988 until 2000, then moving to the Swanage Railway. Sold on again in 2004 to Jeremy Hosking it was moved to Southall and transferred to the Royal Scot Locomotive and General Trust in early 2011, moving again to Ian Riley's works at Bury for restoration to mainline standard.

British Railways (Southern Region) rebuilt Bulleid 'Merchant Navy' Class 4-6-2 No. 35029 *Ellerman Lines* restarts from Basingstoke station while in charge of the southbound 'Pines Express' on the afternoon of Saturday 22 May 1965.

The 'Pines Express' was introduced in 1910, though it was an un-named train until September 1927; it ran originally via the Somerset & Dorset Joint Line, where it was the most prestigious train. Its final run via the S&DJR was on 8 September 1962, hauled by Standard 9F 2-10-0 No. 92220 *Evening Star*, after which it was diverted to run via Southampton, Basingstoke, Reading and Oxford. The SR loco usually worked the train to Oxford and back, as it did in this case. From 4 October 1965 the train was extended to run to Poole, but the service finished from 4 March 1967.

No. 35029 was built at Eastleigh Works in February 1949 and over its lifetime was allocated to Bournemouth, Dover, Nine Elms and Weymouth, being rebuilt at Eastleigh in September 1959. Withdrawn in September 1966 it was stored at Nine Elms and Weymouth before ending up at Woodham's, Barry by March 1967. It became part of the National Collection in January 1974 after which it was 'sectioned' to show the interior workings and displayed at the National Railway Museum in York.

From the Geoff Plumb Collection of original slides, photographer unknown. Filthy dirty Bulleid rebuilt 'West Country' Class 4-6-2 No. 34048 *Crediton* is brewing up in the down bay platform (I think!) at Salisbury while an express train is stopped on the down main. Porters and passengers go about their business, while the engine crew watch proceedings on a very wet day, possibly around September 1963.

No. 34048 was built at Brighton Works and entered service in November 1946 as No. 21C148, being renumbered at the beginning of BR in 1948. It spent its early SR and BR years at Salisbury shed and Exmouth Junction before moving to Brighton in 1951. After rebuilding at Eastleigh Works in March 1959 it was reallocated to Bournemouth for a short while until early 1960 when it was transferred back to Salisbury, where it remained until withdrawal in March 1966. It was then stored at Eastleigh until July 1966 and a further period was spent stored at Dock Street Goods yard in Newport, finally being scrapped by Cashmore's, Newport, in September 1966.

Southern Railway unrebuilt Bulleid 'West Country' Class 4-6-2 No. 34002 *Salisbury* is at the head of a train in its namesake station at Salisbury on Saturday 9 May 1964, possibly with the 11:10 train from Plymouth to Brighton, which stopped at Salisbury from 14:49 until 14:56. The RCTS 'East Midlander No. 7' Rail Tour, which I was aboard, stopped here from 14:53 to 15:00. Alongside is an unidentified rebuilt Bulleid 'Pacific' with an express bound for Waterloo.

From the Geoff Plumb Collection of original slides, photo by D.E. White. Unrebuilt Bulleid 'Merchant Navy' Class 4-6-2 No. 35003 *Royal Mail* has the road and is raring to go with an up west of England express at Templecombe Joint Station, bound for Waterloo on Friday 2 May 1958.

The engine was built at Eastleigh Works as No. 21C3, entering service during September 1941 and named the following month – it was an Exmouth Junction loco at the time of nationalisation. Rebuilt at Eastleigh during August 1959, it returned to Exmouth Junction until July 1964, then moving in quick succession to Nine Elms and Bournemouth. Transferred again to Weymouth in October 1966 its final re-allocation was to Nine Elms in April 1967, where it lasted until the end of steam in July 1967. It was stored at Weymouth until November 1967 before moving to Cashmore's, Newport, where it was scrapped during December 1967.

From the Geoff Plumb Collection of original slides, photographer unknown. Ex-LSWR M7 class 2P 0-4-4T No. 30254 rubs shoulders with classmate 30251 in the yard at Micheldever, though it doesn't look like either of them is in steam. Date unknown, but probably around June 1963.

No. 30254 spent much of its BR career at Barnstaple Junction MPD but was transferred to Norwood Junction then Bournemouth and Salisbury sheds in 1963, so this photo may have been taken whilst the loco was en route to Bournemouth, or from Bournemouth to Salisbury. Withdrawn in May 1964 it was stored at Salisbury until September, being scrapped by T.W. Ward at Briton Ferry in October 1964.

No. 30251 also spent much of its BR time at Barnstaple Junction before being transferred to Norwood Junction and Feltham in 1963. Its final transfer to Eastleigh also took place in 1963 from where it was withdrawn in July and scrapped by August of the same year, at Eastleigh Works.

Rebuilt 'Merchant Navy' Class 4-6-2 No. 35004 *Cunard White Star* dashes through Micheldever with a down express from Waterloo to Southampton and Bournemouth on Saturday 13 March 1965. Complete with brake van, an engineering train is stabled in the up side siding, possibly with a load of conductor rails as part of the ongoing electrification works.

Built at Eastleigh Works in October 1941, the loco carried its SR number 21C4 and was named in January 1942. Renumbered 35004 in April 1948, it spent its BR career alternating between Exmouth Junction and Salisbury sheds, returning to Salisbury after rebuilding at Eastleigh in July 1958. It was re-allocated to Bournemouth depot from September 1964 and withdrawn in October 1965. Stored at Eastleigh until February 1966 it was cut-up on site at Eastleigh MPD by Cohens.

Having been routed over 'The Alps' via Alton and Medstead, due to engineering works on the main line, rebuilt 'Merchant Navy' Class 'Pacific' No. 35028 *Clan Line* stops for water at Winchester City station whilst at the head of the RCTS 'Somerset & Dorset Farewell' Railtour on Sunday 6 March 1966. The loco seems to be leaking steam from everywhere possible and it looks like there is a serious steam-heating leak further along the train! Later, a stop was made at Branksome to change a steam-pipe. Note the up line has a new conductor rail in place but the down line is still to obtain this, the electrification work to Southampton and Bournemouth still being incomplete.

Photographers scramble around on the cutting side, trying to find the best vantage point during the eleven minute stop from 11.05 to 11:16, the train departing one minute late with 35028 working as far as Templecombe No. 2 Junction, where LMS Ivatt 2MT 2-6-2Ts Nos. 41283 and 41249 take over for the onward leg via Evercreech Junction to Highbridge.

Southern Railway unrebuilt Bulleid 'West Country' class 4-6-2 No. 34038 *Lynton* has arrived alongside the station at Eastleigh on Saturday 9 May 1964 with the RCTS 'East Midlander No.7' Railtour. It had taken over the train at Didcot and was routed via the DN&S line to reach here. The loco came off the train at this point which was then was taken forward into the works area by USATC S100 Class 0-6-0T No. 30071. No. 34038 was then turned and serviced at the shed before hauling the train once more via Salisbury to Swindon Works.

Built at Brighton Works in September 1946, the loco entered service

as 21C138 and was renumbered to 34038 after nationalisation in 1948, during its allocation to Stewarts Lane shed, transferring later in 1948 to Brighton. It became a Plymouth Friary engine from May 1951 until January 1958 when it was re-allocated to Exmouth Junction MPD. Back at Brighton from November 1960 for a year, it became an Eastleigh loco from November 1961 and its final transfer was to Nine Elms in January 1965. It was withdrawn in June 1966 and stored at Nine Elms until September 1966, then going to Cashmore's, Newport, where it was scrapped the same month.

Unrebuilt 'WC' Class 4-6-2 No. 34038 *Lynton* had arrived into Eastleigh from Didcot with the RCTS 'East Midlander No. 7' Railtour on Saturday 9 May 1964 and was taken off the train to go for servicing at the shed. It was replaced by filthy dirty USATC S100 0-6-0T No. 30071 which took the train into the works area for a visit by the tour passengers. The loco is just passing the signal box at the south end of the station.

No. 30071 was built by Vulcan Ironwork (USA), Works No. 4439 of 1943 and worked for the vast majority of its twenty-five year life around Southampton Docks, where its short wheelbase was a necessity. It was transferred to Eastleigh MPD in June 1963 and was withdrawn from there in July 1967. It was stored at Salisbury until March 1968 and was finally scrapped at Cashmore's, Newport, later in March 1968.

From the Geoff Plumb Collection of original slides, photographer unknown, but possibly E.A.S. Cotton. LSWR Adams 'Radial Tank' 4-4-2T Class 0415 No. 30584 sits dumped at Eastleigh depot after withdrawal from service. The date is uncertain, but is most probably a winter afternoon in 1961.

Three locos of the class survived to work the Lyme Regis branch but finally succumbed to progress. This loco and 30582 were scrapped, but 30583 was preserved on the Bluebell Railway. Alongside is 'Lord Nelson' Class 4-6-0 No. 30855 *Robert Blake*, also awaiting its fate.

No. 30584 was built as works number 2109 by Dübs, Glasgow, in 1885, and was withdrawn from Exmouth Junction shed in February 1961. It was scrapped at Eastleigh Works in December 1961. No. 30855 was built at Eastleigh Works in 1928 and was withdrawn from Eastleigh shed in September 1961, also being scrapped at Eastleigh in February 1962.

From the Geoff Plumb Collection of original slides, photographer unknown, but possibly E.A.S. Cotton. N15 'King Arthur' Class 4-6-0 No. 30772 *Sir Percivale* catches the last of the evening sunshine as it awaits its fate on the scrap line at Eastleigh depot. This was one of thirty engines built by North British Locomotive Co., Glasgow, and entered service during June 1925. Its final allocation was to Bournemouth MPD from June 1957 and it was withdrawn from there in September 1961, then making its way to Eastleigh where it was scrapped during December 1961, presumably soon after this photo was taken.

From the Geoff Plumb Collection of original slides, photographer unknown, but possibly E.A.S. Cotton. LSWR Adams 'Radial Tank' 4-4-2T class 0415 No. 30582 is dumped at Eastleigh depot after withdrawal from service, one of three that outlived their classmates by many years to work the Lyme Regis branch. The date is uncertain, but is most probably a winter afternoon in 1961. This loco and 30584 were scrapped, but 30583 was preserved on the Bluebell Railway. Behind is 'Lord Nelson' Class 4-6-0 No. 30855 *Robert Blake*, also awaiting its fate, and various locos can be seen in the yard beyond. No. 30582 was built by Robert Stephenson & Co. in 1885, with works number 2608, and was withdrawn from Exmouth Junction shed in July 1961. It was scrapped at Eastleigh Works in March 1962.

South Eastern and Chatham Railway Wainwright Class H 0-4-4T No. 31522, built in 1909 at Ashford Works. No. 31522 has reached the end of the line on the scrap road at Eastleigh Works on Saturday 2 February 1963 and stripping has just commenced. This was one of the locos fitted with Autotrain 'Push-Pull' equipment from 1949. One member of the class, No. 31263, survived into preservation. No. 31522 was withdrawn from Tunbridge Wells West shed in January 1963 and arrived at Eastleigh later the same month and was scrapped during February 1963. Behind is an unidentified Class Z 0-8-0T, possibly No. 30954, also in the early stages of stripping for scrap. These locos had been mainly used for trip workings around south London and banking trains between Exeter St. David's and Exeter Central, up the 1 in 37 graded line.

From the Geoff Plumb Collection of original slides, photographer unknown. SR unrebuilt Bulleid 'West Country' Class 4-6-2 No. 34038 *Lynton* has just hauled the RCTS 'East Midlander No. 7' Railtour from Didcot via the DN&S line on Saturday 9 May 1964, and is still carrying the RCTS headboard (though not the 'East Midlander' headboard) as it is serviced at Eastleigh MPD. It has already been turned to take the tour onwards via Salisbury to Swindon Works.

Maunsell SR Class S15 4-6-0 No. 30824 simmers on shed at Eastleigh MPD between duties on Saturday 9 May 1964, with the huge water tower cum office block behind. The headcode it is carrying suggests it has arrived from Basingstoke as a light engine.

The loco was built at Eastleigh and entered service in March 1927; when BR was formed in January 1948, the engine was allocated to Exmouth Junction, moving to Salisbury in June 1951. It remained there until reallocated to Feltham during the month ending on 6 January 1964 and it is carrying that shed's 70B code in this picture. It changed depots again at the end of 1964, at least on paper, to Eastleigh, but was stored at Feltham, finally moving to Eastleigh in July 1965. It was withdrawn in September 1965 – still at Feltham – and stored until November 1965, finally ending up at Cashmore's, Newport, where it was scrapped during December 1965.

BR Standard 4MT 2-6-4T No. 80012 is newly ex-works in fully lined black livery, simmering in the shed yard at Eastleigh MPD on Saturday 9 May 1964. It is not carrying a shedcode plate but it has SR style lamp irons, so is a Southern Region loco.

The engine was built at Brighton Works and entered service during August 1951, initially allocated to Tunbridge Wells West MPD. It remained a Southern Region engine all its life of nearly sixteen years

and was a Feltham engine at this time. It was transferred to Eastleigh in November 1964, and its final move was to Nine Elms in October 1965, from where it was withdrawn in March 1967. Stored at Nine Elms until July 1967, it then moved to Salisbury for further storage until August 1967 and was eventually scrapped by Buttigieg's, Newport, the following month.

Unrebuilt Bulleid 'Battle of Britain' Class 4-6-2 No. 34064 *Fighter Command* has just gone through the works at Eastleigh and sits in its resplendent paintwork outside the shed at Eastleigh, coaled up ready for work, on Saturday 9 May 1964.

The engine was built at Brighton Works, the 1,000th loco built there, emerging as 21C164 in July 1947. It was also the first SR Pacific to be built with a 'vee' shaped cab, and went to Ramsgate depot and then Stewarts Lane. From 1950 it was allocated to Nine Elms depot and it carried experimental apple green livery from June 1948 to June 1950 as part of the BR livery trials. Some three years were spent allocated to Exmouth Junction until mid-1962 when it returned to Nine Elms.

The Giesl Ejector was fitted in April 1962 and did enhance the engine's performance considerably, but as with so many such improvements it came too late to make a real difference for the class. The loco was reallocated to Eastleigh in late 1963 and moved on to Salisbury from 25 October 1965. It was withdrawn in May 1966 and stored at Basingstoke Yard for a few months before being scrapped at Bird's, Bridgend, during November 1966.

Southern Railway Urie S15 Class 4-6-0 No. 30512 sits on the scrap line at Eastleigh MPD on Saturday 9 May 1964, and although it was later moved to Woodham's at Barry it did not survive into preservation. Behind is an unidentified unrebuilt Bulleid Pacific, its nameplate removed and coat of arms crudely cut out from its air-smoothed casing.

30512 was built at Eastleigh Works and entered service in February 1921. It was allocated to Feltham MPD for its entire BR career and was withdrawn in March 1964. It was moved to Eastleigh until November 1964 and then sold to Woodham's at Barry. Unlike most engines that ended up there, it was scrapped in January 1965.

LSWR B4 Class 0-4-0T No. 30102 was one of the engines used on the docks in Southampton (where it acquired the name *Granville*) and has now sadly reached the scrap line at Eastleigh engine shed on Saturday 9 May 1964, sandwiched between two LBSCR Class A1X 'Terrier Tank' 0-6-0Ts Nos. 32662 and 32650. Happily, all three of these engines were bought for preservation and survive to this day.

No. 30102 was built at Nine Elms Works and entered service during December 1893. Its BR service began at Eastleigh from early 1948 and it then moved to Plymouth Friary in 1949 until July 1958 when it moved back to Eastleigh for a short time and then to Bournemouth until around October 1961. It then made its final reallocation back to Eastleigh from where it was withdrawn in September 1963 and stored until October 1964. The loco was initially sold to Butlin's and displayed at the Ayr Holiday Camp until 1971, when it was acquired by Bressingham Museum near Diss, Norfolk, for preservation.

Southern Railway Maunsell Class Q 0-6-0 No. 30548 is out of use at Eastleigh MPD, together with a Bulleid Q1 Class 0-6-0 on the left and a BR Standard 4MT 2-6-0 on the right, on Saturday 9 May 1964. No. 30548 was built at Eastleigh Works and entered service during August 1939 as No. 548. It spent most of its BR career allocated to Bournemouth shed with short periods at Stewarts Lane and Three Bridges.

It was reallocated to Eastleigh at the beginning of 1963 and withdrawn from there in March 1965, so was theoretically still in service at the time of this photo. After withdrawal, it was stored at Eastleigh until June1965 and was eventually scrapped at Cox & Danks, Park Royal, during July 1965. This was one of the class fitted with the Lemaître multiple blast-pipe and associated large diameter chimney. Classmate No. 30541 survived into preservation, and is based on the Bluebell Railway.

On the scrap road at Eastleigh MPD a couple of young spotters have just 'cabbed' B4 Class 0-4-0T No. 30102, which is surrounded by 'Terrier' 0-6-0Ts of Class A1X on Saturday 9 May 1964. On the left is No. 32662; the main subject is 32650 while on the right is 32646. Fortunately, all these engines survived into preservation.

No. 32650 was built at Brighton Works, entering service during December 1876 as LBSCR No. 50 *Whitechapel*, and began a long and complicated career. It was renumbered 650 in 1901 then became Southern Railway No. B650 in the grouping of 1923. In 1930 it was shipped over to the Isle of Wight and became No. W9 *Fishbourne*, remaining there until 1936. It then returned to the mainland where it was renumbered 515S to be used as a shunter at Lancing Carriage Works, becoming DS515 under BR. It worked at Lancing until 1953 when it was swapped with another 'Terrier' to work on the Hayling Island branch as it had a larger bunker as a result of its sojourn on the

Isle of Wight – it was then renumbered to 32650 and was based at Fratton shed. It worked the Hayling Island line for the next ten years and hauled the final working on the line, the 21:00 on Sunday 2 November 1963. By this time the engine was allocated to Eastleigh and along with the other remaining engines of the class was withdrawn in November 1963 and stored.

In 1964 the Borough of Sutton & Cheam wanted to purchase fellow 'Terrier' No. 61 *Sutton* and put it on display, but unfortunately this loco had already been scrapped, so the decision was made to buy 32650 instead and preserve it as *Sutton*. After the loco was bought, it was moved to the Kent & East Sussex Railway for restoration and use, provided it kept the name *Sutton*. The engine was restored to working order by 1969 and hauled the line's official first train in 1974. Later, the engine was moved to the Spa Valley Railway, Tunbridge Wells, though still under the ownership of the Sutton Borough Council.

This USATC S100 Class 3F 0-6-0T No. 30073 was repainted into a BR
version of Southern Railway malachite green livery during the latter
part of its service. It is seen here in steam between duties on shed at
Eastleigh MPD on Saturday 9 May 1964, with a young enthusiast in the
cab.

No. 30073 (Works No. 4447) was one of fifteen acquired by the
Southern Railway in 1943 (thirteen of them including this engine built
by Vulcan Iron Works in Wilkes-Barre, USA, in 1942, the two others built
by Porter of Pittsburgh). One of the fifteen was used as spares for the
other class members. Various adaptions had to be made for their use in
Britain and this took until November 1947 for all the engines to be in
service, originally around Southampton Docks to replace the old B4, D1
and E1 tank engines previously employed. Their short wheelbase was

ideal but their austerity construction meant they did not wear well, the
steel fireboxes presenting problems by 1951 when several locos
required new fireboxes.

Nevertheless, they continued until 1962 when they were replaced by
new BR Class 07 diesel shunters. Six of the locos received Departmental
numbers to work at Meldon Quarry, Redbridge Sleeper Works, BR
Ashford Works and Lancing Carriage Works, others taking on 'general
duties' such as shed pilots. No. 30073 was one of these, and transferred
to Eastleigh on 24 June 1963 from where it was withdrawn in December
1966. It was stored at Eastleigh until April 1967, before moving for a
short period to Salisbury until May 1967, and then on to Cashmore's
Newport, where it was scrapped during June 1967. Four members of
the class have survived into preservation.

Southern Railway Maunsell S15 Class 4-6-0 No. 30836 has just arrived 'on shed' at Eastleigh MPD on Saturday 9 May 1964, carrying a headcode that suggests a light engine working to Eastleigh from west of Basingstoke. Behind is BR Standard 4MT 2-6-4T No. 80012 which has just been through the works and newly repainted.

No. 30836 was built at Eastleigh Works and entered service in December 1927. At the start of BR it was allocated to Feltham shed but spent most of its BR career at Redhill before returning to Feltham in June 1963 and it is carrying that shed's code of 70B in this photo. It was withdrawn from service just a few weeks after the picture was taken and was scrapped at Cashmore's, Newport during October 1964.

Southern Railway N Class 2-6-0 No. 31811 awaits its fate on the scrap road at Eastleigh depot on Sunday 25 July 1965, together with U Class No. 31790 and an unidentified Bulleid 'Pacific'. No. 31811 was built at Ashford Works and entered service in June 1920; it spent its early BR years allocated to Stewarts Lane before being transferred to Guildford in May/June 1959. It had just been withdrawn from service and was stored at Eastleigh until October 1965, then made its final journey to Buttigieg's, Newport, where it was scrapped in November 1965.

Bulleid Q1 Class 0-6-0 No. 33018 looks as though it may have been in use recently as its wheels only have superficial rust on them, but it may now have been dumped. It is standing in front of an unidentified LMS Ivatt 2-6-2T and a BR Standard 2-6-4T at Eastleigh shed on Sunday 25 July 1965.

No. 33018 was built at Ashford Works and entered service as SR No.

C18 in April 1942. It led a fairly nomadic career, ending up transferred from Guildford to Nine Elms in June 1965 and withdrawn just a few weeks later. Storage at Eastleigh followed until September 1965, the engine then moving to Cashmore's, Newport, where it was scrapped during December 1965.

Southern Railway rebuilt Bulleid 'Merchant Navy' Class 4-6-2 No. 35023 *Holland–Afrika Line* has the road and is raring to go, but the water column 'bag' is still in the tender, replenishing the water supply as it waits to leave Southampton Central station with the down 'Bournemouth Belle' from Waterloo. A friend and I had travelled down from Waterloo on Tuesday 27 October 1964 and enjoyed a splendid lunch (we were fifteen years old at the time!) but couldn't afford to travel any further at Pullman rates. Note the dockyard cranes in the background; the large funnel just visible on the left above the driver's greasetop cap belongs to RMS *Queen Elizabeth*, then still in service.

The tender tank has been refilled and the fire, glimpsed through the cab door, is almost white-hot as the driver climbs aboard 'Merchant Navy' Class 4-6-2 No. 35023 *Holland–Afrika Line*, prior to departing from Southampton Central station with the down 'Bournemouth Belle' Pullman train from Waterloo to Bournemouth, on Tuesday 27 October 1964.

No. 35023 was built at Eastleigh Works and entered service from November 1948, spending the first twelve years of its career at Exmouth Junction shed, during which time it was rebuilt at Eastleigh Works in February 1957. By March 1960 it had moved on to Bournemouth Depot where it remained until October 1966, transferring again to Weymouth until April 1967. Its final re-allocation was to Nine Elms, from where it was withdrawn at the end of steam in July 1967. Stored at Nine Elms and then Salisbury until March 1968, it ended up at Buttigieg's, Newport, and was scrapped during April 1968.

One of the SR built Solent paddle steamers, PS *Ryde*, arrives at Ryde Pier Head with a sailing from Portsmouth and Southsea, July 1969. She was built by Denny of Dumbarton and launched in April 1937 and was taken over by the Royal Navy during the Second World War, mainly acting as a minesweeper in the Thames estuary and Dover straits along with sister ship PS *Sandown*. Both ships were involved in the Dunkirk evacuations and D-Day landings before returning to their ferry and excursion work in the Solent. Withdrawn from service in 1969, PS *Ryde* became a night-club venue near Newport as the *Ryde Queen* for some years before being sunk as a precaution at her moorings and later 'beached'.

London & South Western Railway O2 Class 0P 0-4-4T No. W31 *Chale* was one of the engines fitted with a Drummond boiler (with the safety valves on the dome), and is here waiting to depart from Ryde Pier Head with the 16:08 train to Ventnor on the afternoon of Thursday 3 September 1964. The O2s were another very long-lived class of engines, partly because few other classes were suited to working on the Isle of Wight, though a few lasted into the 1960s on the mainland as well.

Designed by W. Adams, this engine was built at Nine Elms Works, one of sixty locos, and entered service as LSWR No. 180 in April 1890,

being renumbered to E180 by the SR in May 1924, when it also gained Maunsell lined green livery. Moved to the Isle of Wight in May 1927 it became No. W31, fitted with Westinghouse brake equipment. The engines all received enlarged coal bunkers from 1932, this one being the last modified in 1936. It was allocated to Newport shed until November 1957, then moving to Ryde St. John's until withdrawal in March 1967 after the island line was electrified – it was used during the electrification works. Stored at Ryde until August 1967, it was moved to Sollife, Newport IoW, and scrapped there during September 1967.

Ex-London & South Western Railway O2 Class 0-4-4T No. W14 *Fishbourne* starts the 15:28 to Ventnor on Sunday 30 August 1964, away from a busy Ryde Pier Head station, while another O2 runs round its train to form a working to Cowes. PS *Ryde* has recently arrived with a sailing from Southsea, the paddle steamer then in BR Southern Region livery of black hull with white upperworks and yellow funnel. In the foreground is the pier tramway, then still in operation.

Built at Nine Elms Works in December 1889 the loco entered service as No. 178, the second of the class. Renumbered E178 by the SR in August 1926 it reverted to 178 in November 1932 before moving to the IoW in May 1936 to become W14, allocated to Ryde St. John's during the BR era. After a service life of 77 years and covering almost 1½ million miles, it was withdrawn in December 1966 when the island lines closed and the Ryde–Shanklin section was electrified. Stored at Newport until April 1967, it was scrapped at Sollife, Newport IoW, in May 1967.

O2 Class 0-4-4T No. W24 *Calbourne* drifts into Ryde Esplanade station at the landward end of Ryde Pier, having just left Pier Head with the 14:28 train to Ventnor on a glorious sunny Sunday 30 August 1964. These engines didn't carry the 'W' prefix to their numbers, except on a small numberplate on the rear of the bunker.

Nine Elms Works built the loco as No. 209 in December 1891 and after early years at Fratton and Exeter it was moved to the IoW on 26 April 1925, becoming W24. Its entire BR career was spent allocated to

Ryde St. John's Road depot, from where it was withdrawn in March 1967 after electrification work on the Ryde–Shanklin section was completed. Stored at Ryde until August 1969 it was sold for preservation to the Wight Locomotive Society, forerunners to the Isle of Wight Steam Railway, based at Haven Street, where it has been operational. This engine is the sole survivor of the class and has recently undergone another rebuild.

O2 Class 0P 0-4-4T No. W35 *Freshwater* stands at Ryde Esplanade station with the 14:34 train from Ryde Pier Head to Cowes on Sunday 30 August 1964. It is hot on the heels of W24 *Calbourne* with the 14:28 train to Ventnor and is now having to wait the road.

A product of Nine Elms Works in May 1890, numbered 181, it became No. E181 in June 1926, reverting to 181 in April 1933. Based at Wadebridge during early BR days as No. 30181, though whether it carried this number is uncertain, it was transferred to Newport on the Isle of Wight during early 1949, becoming W35, and then moved to Ryde depot in 1956. It was withdrawn from service in October 1966 and stored at Newport until April 1967; it was scrapped at Sollife, Newport, in May 1967.

O2 Class 0-4-4T No. W29 *Alverstone* is still carrying duty board 12 though it is not in steam as it sits outside the shed at Ryde St. John's Road on Thursday 22 July 1965.

This engine was built at Nine Elms Works in July 1891 and entered service as LSWR No. 202. It was renumbered E202 after the formation of the Southern Railway in 1923 and renumbered again to W29 in April 1926 after shipping to the Isle of Wight. Its home base was Newport shed until early 1957 when it migrated to Ryde for the remainder of its career, being withdrawn from there in May 1966. It was stored there until August 1966 then moved across to the Works, where it was scrapped in May 1967.

A couple of O2 Class 0-4-4Ts simmer on shed at Ryde St. John's Road between duties on a lovely summer's day, Sunday 30 August 1964. On the left is No. W16 *Ventnor*, while on the right is W21 *Sandown*. Both engines were products of Nine Elms Works as Nos. 217 of June 1892 and 205 of September 1891 respectively.

No. 217 arrived on the IoW in May 1936 to become W16, while 205 became W21 on arrival on the island in June 1924. W21 was withdrawn from service in May 1966 and was stored at Ryde shed until August when it moved to the adjacent Works, being scrapped there during May 1967. W16 lasted until the end of steam on the island in December 1966 and then was stored at Newport until April 1967, followed by dismantling by Sollife, Newport, in May 1967.

O2 Class 0-4-4T No.W14 *Fishbourne* is carrying a single white disc on the top lamp bracket, denoting a train for Ventnor. This is the 10:28 from Ryde Pier Head between Ryde St. John's Road station and Smallbrook Junction (Smallbrook Lane Bridge), on Tuesday 1 September 1964. During the busy summer months when Smallbrook Junction signal box was manned, this section was operated as double track; in quieter periods when it was not necessary for the signal box to be open, this section was operated as two single tracks, one for the Ventnor line and one for the Cowes line.

O2 Class 0P 0-4-4T No. W33 *Bembridge* is approaching Brading station with the 18:25 train from Ryde Pier Head to Ventnor on a lovely summer evening, on Tuesday 20 July 1965. The train is just passing the point where the former branch line to Bembridge curved off to the right, this line closing to passengers from 21 September 1953.

The loco was outshopped from Nine Elms Works in August 1892 as

No. 218, becoming E218 in September 1926 under the SR's auspices then was renumbered to W33 on moving to the IoW in May 1936. In early BR days it was a Newport engine, transferring to Ryde St. John's Road shed in November 1957, remaining there until the end of Isle of Wight steam in December 1966. It was stored at Newport from January to April 1967 and scrapped by Sollife, Newport, in May 1967.

O2 class 0-4-4T No. W31 *Chale* comes into Brading station with the 18:05 train from Ryde Pier Head to Ventnor. The loco was one of the class members fitted with a Drummond boiler, the safety valves situated on the dome. It has now had its nameplates removed but still looks in reasonable condition on the lovely summer evening of Tuesday 20 July 1965.

Brading was the junction station for the Bembridge branch which was officially opened on 27 May 1882, after a prolonged construction period which included reclaiming land from the Eastern Yar river estuary on which to build the railway. As with many branch lines, it eventually suffered from the encroaching road transport, the last passenger train running on 20 September 1953, though goods trains still ran to St. Helens Quay until November 1957, when the track was lifted.

0-4-4T Class O2 No. W16 *Ventnor* has just set off from Brading station on the double track section southwards towards Sandown with the 09:28 Ryde Pier Head to Ventnor train on the lovely morning of Monday 31 August 1964. Note the unfenced public footpath alongside the track from a local road (Yarbridge) to the station! The footpath is still there, though these days it is fenced-off from the electrified lines.

In a picture taken from the footpath alongside the line to Brading station, on Monday 19 July 1965, No. W24 *Calbourne* storms away from the station with a morning extra train from Ryde Pier Head to Ventnor. W24 had recently been through works and repainted in unlined black livery and without its nameplates, but survived into preservation.

Dumped in the Chalk Siding is W32 *Bonchurch*, also shorn of its nameplates. This engine was withdrawn in October 1964 and has

obviously been there for some time, though ostensibly stored at Ryde St. John's Road shed. It was later returned to Ryde Works, where it was scrapped during October 1965. It was built at Nine Elms Works as No. 226 in November 1892, becoming E226 in March 1925 and transferred to the Isle of Wight in May 1928 to take the number W32. Early BR days were spent at Newport shed and reallocation to Ryde happened in November 1957.

Seen from Gills (or Jeals?) Footbridge over the cutting just north of Sandown station, O2 Class 0P 0-4-4T No. W21 *Sandown* is approaching the station of the same name on the double track section from Brading with a train from Ryde Pier Head to Ventnor on Saturday 24 July 1965.

Note the track ballast is formed of shingle rather than granite chippings as used on much of the mainland. As in so many locations, the area around this photo is now much built-up with housing – the railway is now just single track between Brading and Sandown.

O2 Class 0-4-4T No. W14 *Fishbourne* is heading south between Sandown and Shanklin with the 10:28 train from Ryde Pier Head to Ventnor on Wednesday 2 September 1964. The photo is taken from Araluen Way running parallel with the railway – this is now the location of Lake Halt which was officially opened on 9 July 1987, though it had been in use from the previous May!

The original Lake Halt was slightly further south, opened in 1889 to serve the County Cricket Ground (now the Shanklin Football Club) and a convalescent home; it was closed in 1914. On an almost continuous climb at varying gradients from Sandown to Shanklin, No. W14 is working quite hard on the 1 in 88 at this point.

O2 Class 0-4-4T No. W21 *Sandown* is hard at work with a nice clean fire as it climbs the 1 in 70 gradient of Apse Bank from Shanklin near Upper Hyde, en route to Wroxall and Ventnor with the 12:08 limited stop train from Ryde Pier Head on Saturday 29 August 1964. It will soon pass the site of an old siding, known as Apse siding, built in 1868 to serve a quarry. It was of very light construction and prohibited to locomotives; also special permission had to be obtained to shunt it as it was on the steep gradient.

O2 Class 0-4-4T No. W22 *Brading* has just breasted the 1 in 70 climb of Apse Bank from Shanklin but is still working hard with a nice clean fire on the lesser gradient of 1 in 228 at this point. It is in charge of the 11:28 train on Saturday 29 August 1964 from Ryde Pier Head to Ventnor, now well on its way to Wroxall at Three Arch Bridge. In the far background the white outcrop of Culver Cliffs marks the northern side of Sandown Bay.

Built at Nine Elms Works in June 1892, the engine entered service as LSWR No. 215 and later became E215 on the formation of the Southern Railway after the grouping in 1923. It came to the Isle of Wight in June 1924 where it was renumbered W22. At the time of the picture, it was one of the engines fitted with a Drummond boiler. It spent its BR career shedded at Ryde St. John's Road from where it was withdrawn at the end of steam running in December 1966. Stored at Newport until April 1967, it met its end at Sollife, Newport, during May 1967.

O2 Class 0-4-4T No. W30 *Shorwell* has just passed under Three Arch Bridge after climbing the 1 in 70 Apse Bank, almost one and a quarter miles long, from Shanklin en route to Wroxall and Ventnor whilst working duty No. 4. This is the 11:08 departure from Ryde Pier Head to Ventnor on Saturday 29 August 1964. The gradient eased to 1 in 228 along this section before increasing again to 1 in 113 on the approach to Wroxall, so quite a trial for southbound trains. This area was noted for the presence of adders – though I didn't find that out until later! On 12 August 1940, several bombs landed near here, one explosion causing damage to the track though other bombs failed to explode. The line was closed for ten days whilst the track and embankment were repaired.

O2 Class 0-4-4T No. W30 *Shorwell* now returns from Ventnor with the 12:20 train for Ryde Pier Head, passing the grazing cattle between Wroxall and Shanklin at Three Arch Bridge on Saturday 29 August 1964. Turned out from Nine Elms Works in September 1892, the engine was originally numbered 219 until gaining the 'E' prefix under the Southern Railway after 1923.

It became an Isle of Wight engine from April 1926 and was renumbered W30. Its early BR days saw it based at Newport, moving to Ryde in November 1957. It was withdrawn in September 1965, presumably after the end of the summer season, and stored until November 1965 when it was scrapped at Ryde Works.

O2 Class 0-4-4T No. W21 *Sandown* has arrived at Ventnor station with the 11:28 train from Ryde Pier Head and is now taking water in the course of running round its train, before returning to Ryde as the 12:40 departure, on Wednesday 2 September 1964. There is still plenty of evidence of coal traffic to the merchants in the station yard, also storage areas in the caves in the cliffside. The 1,312 yards long tunnel through St Boniface Down can just be seen to the left of the coach in the platform.

The station was built on the site of a quarry dating from around 1841 and, apparently, the caves were excavated by prisoners from the Napoleonic wars. The site continued to enlarge with further excavations until 1923. Although a useful site, it was 276 feet above sea-level, so quite a climb for intending passengers from the town! Opened in 1866, the station was closed one hundred years later on Sunday 17 April 1966 when services south of Shanklin ceased.

London and South Western Railway O2 Class 0-4-4T No. W17 *Seaview* has run round its train and is now preparing to return to Ryde Pier Head with the 11:40 working on Sunday 30 August 1964. The fireman is using the slacking hose on the coal to damp down the dust from bunker-first running, especially in the cramped confines of the tunnel under St Boniface Down, just beyond the signal box. Note the cover over the Westinghouse brake pump on the side of the smokebox – this was to prevent passengers waiting on platforms from being sprayed with hot, oily water as the pumps worked to replenish brake air pressure as trains came to a stop at stations.

No. W17 was built at Nine Elms Works and entered service as LSWR No. 208 in December 1891 then was renumbered to E208 in July 1924 after the formation of the Southern Railway in 1923. Moved to the Isle of Wight, it became No. W17 in May 1930. Despite its rather tatty looking state here, it survived until the end of steam on the island in December 1966, a service life of 75 years. It was stored at Newport (IoW) from January until April 1967 and scrapped there by Sollife during May 1967.

O2 Class 0-4-4T No.W35 *Freshwater* is working the 11:30 train from Ryde Pier Head to Cowes, seen here between Smallbrook Junction and Ashey on Thursday 22 July 1965. It has just gone under the Whitefield Road Bridge (later the Ashey Road Bridge, also known as the 'Long Arch') on what was originally the Ryde & Newport Railway, opened in December 1875. This became part of the Isle of Wight Central Railway in 1887 and passed into Southern Railway ownership in 1923. Closed by British Railways from 20 February 1966, it is now part of the Isle of Wight Steam Railway with its headquarters at Haven Street.

No. W35 is carrying the Cowes line headcode of two 'white' discs, one above each buffer. Cowes trains normally comprised four coaches, but this one has five, so perhaps a particularly busy day! The coaching stock on the island was almost as ancient as the locomotives, with much of it being former LCDR, LBSCR and SECR bogie carriages, though by this time it was mainly stock from the latter two. These coaches had replaced even older stock over many years.

Under a dramatic summer sky, O2 0-4-4T No. W21 *Sandown* trundles through the landscape having just passed through Ashey station with the daily (as required) 11:09 goods train from Newport to Ryde St John's Road on Thursday 22 July 1965. Much of the load of the goods trains was coal, which was imported by ship from the mainland to Medina Wharf, on the river south of Cowes, and reached by a branch line from north of Newport. Some of the coal was used for firing the locomotives but there were still several coal merchants based at various station yards around the island. The wharf was also where rolling stock and locomotives were delivered to the island, and where exports, such as sugar beet, sailed from. Although passenger services ceased on the Cowes line from 20 February 1966, goods traffic (including materials for the electrification of the Ryde to Shanklin line) from Medina Wharf continued until 24 October 1966.

O2 Class 0-4-4T No. W22 *Brading* drifts towards Ashey station with the 10:24 train from Cowes to Ryde Pier Head on Monday 31 August 1964. Now that classmate No. W24 *Calbourne* has been restored to working order in BR black livery, this is a scene that can be enjoyed again on the Isle of Wight Steam Railway.

Though more or less in the middle of nowhere, Ashey station remained open until passenger services ceased on the line in February 1966. Originally there was a passing loop but the main track had been removed some years earlier, leaving what was the loop and a basic platform in use. The station house had become derelict but is now returned to use as a private house. A siding which went off to the left of this picture led to Ashey Quarry, on a gradient of 1 in 27. The quarry supplied ballast for use on the line and was opened in 1875, but had closed by the end of the century. The siding saw further use when a racecourse was opened to the south of Ashey station in 1882 – special trains were shunted into the siding and the occupants could watch the races from the carriages! The racecourse survived until 1930, when the main grandstand burnt down.

Trains cross at Havenstreet station (originally Haven Street until June 1958) – on the right is O2 No. W33 *Bembridge* which had arrived first with the 16:34 train from Ryde Pier Head to Cowes. On the left is the 16:24 train from Cowes having arrived soon after with W28 *Ashey* in charge. A busy scene ensues prior to both trains departing on Friday 4 September 1964, the station then returning to its slumbers. Similar scenes can be witnessed here today as it is now the headquarters of the Isle of Wight Steam Railway.

The station was originally a small halt opened in 1876 with just a single platform – a siding was added after a gas works was built alongside the station in 1886, though this closed in 1920. When the line was absorbed into the Southern Railway it was decided to increase the service, so a new passing loop was needed and this was built at Haven Street, along with a new island platform, station buildings and signal box during 1926.

O2 0-4-4T No. W20 *Shanklin* has just emerged from the short tunnel on Friday 23 July 1965 as it approaches the bridge over the River Medina on the way into Newport with the 12:30 train from Ryde Pier Head to Cowes. Just behind the camera position the line from Sandown (and also from Ventnor West) via Merstone came in from the right; the two single tracks then ran parallel over Newport Quay on the Medina drawbridge into Newport station.

The Sandown line closed in February 1956 and the line to Ventnor West had already gone from 15 September 1952. The Sandown line section of the drawbridge was removed in 1963. After closure and several attempts to reopen the line, the entire railway infrastructure was swept away for a new road scheme – the only remaining structure is the tunnel now partly used as a pedestrian walkway under the new road.

The daily (Monday to Friday) goods train from Medina Wharf to Ryde St John's Road crosses the River Medina bridge over Newport Quay soon after passing through Newport station with its load of coal wagons on Thursday 3 September 1964. The train is hauled by O2 0-4-4T No. W35 *Freshwater*. The bridge originally had an opening section for river traffic to pass and was two parallel single tracks while it also carried the line from Newport to Sandown and Ventnor West via Merstone. The second track drawbridge was removed in 1963, some years after closure of this line, as can be seen by the bricked up section on the abutment on the left of the picture.

No. W17 *Seaview* has just come across the viaduct over the River Medina and is entering Newport station with the 11:30 train from Ryde Pier Head to Cowes on Friday 23 July 1965. After closure of the Ventnor West and Sandown via Merstone lines, the track-work and signalling has been simplified, the imposing bracket signal structure now comprising just one doll and a shunt signal. There was a Newport South Signal box just before the viaduct but this was demolished and replaced by a Ground Frame around 1959. The engine shed was closed from 1957 and the Carriage Paint Shop in 1959.

O2 Class 0P 0-4-4T No. W22 *Brading* has the signal 'off' to depart from Newport station with the 09:34 train from Ryde Pier Head to Cowes on Saturday 29 August 1964. The original station of the Cowes & Newport Railway was a terminus to the left of where the loco is standing, and opened in June 1862. The later station to accommodate the line to Ryde came into use from December 1875.

The Freshwater, Yarmouth & Newport Railway had its own station to the west of the main station from 1913, on the curve that joined the line to Cowes by the North Signal Box (opened in 1888/89), north of the main station. This station closed during 1923, after which Freshwater trains reverted to using the main station via reversal, the line finally closing in September 1953.

Towards the end of the platform, my father Derek Plumb watches as O2 No. W17 *Seaview* returns from Cowes with the 12:30 train to Ryde Pier Head, entering the station at Newport on Friday 23 July 1965. To the left is the bay platform, and several wagons stand in the yard built on the site of the approach to the original station. The curve of the FY&NR came in on the extreme left to meet the Cowes line by the North Signal Box in the background. There was a loop on the curve where locos ran round their trains so they could pull them into the main station as they were not allowed to propel trains into (or out of) the main station. The large building to the right, seen beyond the station running-in name board, was the Locomotive Repair Shop.

O2 class 0-4-4T No. W20 *Shanklin* slows down with its train for the speed limit over the steel girder bridge south of Cement Mills Halt. The train is the 11:24 from Cowes to Ryde Pier Head, heading for Newport on Thursday 3 September 1964. This part of the line is now a cycleway and footpath. The viaduct crosses what was the Cement Mills' Pond (Dodnor Creek reservoir) and is now a nature reserve.

There was a siding into the works from Cement Mills Halt which also had an internal narrow gauge tramway, part of which crossed under the Cowes line north of the halt, in order to access clay pits west of the main line. The works closed in 1943, but the halt that served it, and a local quay on the River Medina, remained open. At one stage, up to three trains a day ran between the Shide Chalk Pits and the cement works – these trains worked by 'Terrier' tank engines due to severe curvature of the sidings.

O2 0-4-4T No. W22 *Brading* has just performed the 'gravity run-round' at Cowes station. Because of restricted space the engine release points were well back up the platform, so the engine propelled the empty stock past the turnout and the handbrake was applied on the coaches. The engine then ran round while the handbrake was released on the stock which then ran by gravity to the bufferstops. The engine then followed the stock and recoupled ready for departure. This is the 12:24 train to Ryde Pier Head on Thursday 3 September 1964. The footbridge did not connect the platforms – it was a public right of way across the station. After closure, the footbridge was dismantled and re-erected at Medstead & Four Marks station on the Mid-Hants Railway (Watercress Line) in Hampshire.

Southern Railway rebuilt 'Merchant Navy' Class 4-6-2 No. 35013 *Blue Funnel* arrives at Bournemouth Central with an express from Weymouth, passing the engine shed on the right on Saturday 13 March 1965. This train combined with the 14:20 from Bournemouth West, which had been hauled by BR Standard 4MT 2-6-0 No. 76009, to form the 14:40 departure for Waterloo. This train can be seen alongside the engine shed having been into the station to pick up passengers and then reversed out of the station with a pilot loco to the siding. Once the Weymouth train was in the station, the pilot loco propelled the Bournemouth West train back into the station to couple up. The engine shed closed at the end of steam operation in July 1967.

Southern Railway rebuilt 'Merchant Navy' Class 4-6-2 No. 35013 *Blue Funnel* starts away from Bournemouth Central station with the 14:40 express to Waterloo on Saturday 13 March 1965. This train started from Weymouth and combined with the 14:20 from Bournemouth West before continuing. Fortunately, it looks as though some trees had recently been cut down, or this shot would not have been possible!

Bournemouth West station was opened in June 1874 for Waterloo trains and was later also the terminus for the Somerset & Dorset Joint line. It was closed from September 1965, supposedly temporarily during electrification works, but it transpired that Central station could handle all the traffic so the closure became permanent. Part of the site is now Bournemouth Traincare Depot.

In scenes typical of tours in those days, passengers mill about on the tracks as rebuilt 'Merchant Navy' Class 4-6-2 No. 35028 *Clan Line* eases the 'special' forward out of the platform at Broadstone Junction. Several draw-ups were necessary to replenish water tanks in the refreshment car and other coaches from the sole supply. It has come off the lines from Poole; those on the right led to Hamworthy Junction and the loco is now standing on the points leading to the Somerset & Dorset Joint line. This was the RCTS 'Somerset & Dorset Farewell' Railtour, which ran on the last day of operation on the line and of the station, on Sunday 6 March 1966.

The station had been opened as New Poole Junction in 1872 as part of the Southampton & Dorchester Railway. The Ringwood line had already closed by May 1964 and the tracks to Hamworthy Junction were lifted later in 1966. Goods traffic continued for a while to Blandford Forum on the S&DJR and also to a fuel depot at West Moors, beyond Wimborne on the Ringwood line. Blandford traffic ceased from 1969 and that through Wimborne in 1977, after which the station site was demolished.

A very run-down looking BR Standard 4MT 2-6-0 No. 76005 is approaching Worgret Junction from the Wareham direction, hauling the 15:19 train from Poole to Weymouth on Sunday 10 April 1966 with a three coach Bulleid set, No. 786, in tow. The rear of the 10mph sign for the speed restriction for the Swanage branch junction can be seen in the bottom left-hand corner of the picture.

No. 76005 was built at Horwich Works and entered service in December 1952, initially allocated to Eastleigh shed. It spent its entire 14½ year life on the Southern Region. At the stage shown here, it was allocated to Bournemouth MPD; its final allocation from October 1965 after spending the previous ten years based at Salisbury. Despite its appearance it lasted until the end of steam in July 1967. It was stored at Salisbury until October 1967, finally being scrapped by Bird's, Morriston, during November 1967.

From the Geoff Plumb Collection of original slides, photo by D.E. White. BR(S) rebuilt Bulleid 'Merchant Navy' Class 4-6-2 No. 35022 *Holland– America Line* crosses over from the platform line at Weymouth station having arrived with a train from Waterloo on Saturday 27 April 1957. The station was in the process of being enlarged and re-signalled at this stage.

The station was opened by the GWR in 1857 and the LSWR had running powers from Dorchester from the outset, together with a small loco depot. Longer excursion platforms were added from around 1957, as in the photo, these later replaced the original platforms. After the LSWR loco shed was closed, SR locos were serviced and based at the former GWR shed, Weymouth Radipole.

From the Geoff Plumb Collection of original slides, photographer unknown. Southern Railway Maunsell S15 class 4-6-0 No. 30844 comes into Seaton Junction station with an up west of England express heading for Waterloo on an unknown date in the early 1960s. Built at Eastleigh Works as SR No. 844, the loco entered service in October 1936, being renumbered 30844 in August 1950, 2½ years after nationalisation. It spent the majority of its BR career at Exmouth Junction shed until transfer to Feltham in August 1963. Withdrawn in June 1964 it was stored at Feltham until around December 1964 before ending up at Woodham's Barry, where it became one of the few engines scrapped there in January 1965.

Originally named 'Colyton for Seaton', the station opened in July 1860 and was renamed 'Colyton Junction' when the Seaton & Beer Railway (which never reached Beer) opened in March 1868, finally becoming 'Seaton Junction' in June 1869. The station was rebuilt during 1928 to incorporate two through lines as well as the platforms for main line trains and the branch trains. The branch closed to freight in February 1964 and to passengers from 7 March 1966, the station closing from the same date. The main line was reduced to a single track from June 1967, though the main station building, platforms and footbridges still survive. There are now moves afoot to re-double the track and to re-open the station.

From the Geoff Plumb Collection of original slides, photographer unknown. One of the three surviving LSWR Beattie 'Well Tanks', Class 0298 2-4-0WT 0P, No. 30586 is busy doing some shunting in the yard at Wadebridge station on an unknown date in the late 1950s or early 1960s. This loco differed from the two others in that it had square splashers as opposed to rounded. The other two locos survived into preservation, but sadly, not this one. The loco was built by Beyer, Peacock & Co. in October 1875, Works Number 1538, becoming LSWR No. 329. Along with the other two survivors, it spent its entire BR career at Wadebridge. All three were withdrawn in December 1962 after which 30586 was stored at Fratton until March 1963, and then moving to Nine Elms. Its final move was to Eastleigh in July 1963, where it was eventually scrapped in March 1964.

The original Wadebridge station was opened in 1834, one of the earliest stations in the country, as a terminus of the Bodmin & Wadebridge Railway. It was replaced by a new station in 1888 but remained a terminus until the North Cornwall Railway was extended to Padstow in 1899 when it was rebuilt for through workings. The final passenger services ran on 28 January 1967, though freight from Bodmin continued until 1978. Much of the route from Wenfordbridge and Bodmin through Wadebridge to Padstow is now the 'Camel Trail' and both the station building and goods shed at Wadebridge survive, now with new uses.